Simul...
Strat...
Teaching American Government

H O L T

American Government

HOLT, RINEHART AND WINSTON

A Harcourt Education Company

Austin • Orlando • Chicago • New York • Toronto • London • San Diego

ISBN 0-03-066653-8

3 4 5 6 7 8 9 179 04 03

CONTENTS

SIMULATIONS AND STRATEGIES

Simulations and Strategies for Teaching American Government provides a comprehensive collection of creative in-depth activities designed to supplement teacher instruction in the area of American Government. There is one five-page activity for each chapter in the textbook. Each activity in *Simulations and Strategies for Teaching American Government* may be used in combination with teacher-directed lessons for the chapter, as a performance-based assessment of content mastery, or as an enrichment project. All activities in this booklet reflect the following general format.

- **Goal** Each activity begins with a statement of the general learning goal that students will achieve by completing the activity.

- **Overview** This section presents a general overview of the activity by describing the activity's various components.

- **Objectives** This is a listing of the specific learning and performance objectives that students will achieve by completing the activity.

- **Learning Connections** The Learning Connections section of the activity lists the learning styles and critical-thinking skills that will be exercised by the activity and connects the concepts, ideas, and topics covered in the activity to prior learning.

- **Planning** The Planning section of the activity provides the teacher with a wealth of information about the logistics and mechanics of the activity. This information includes the purpose of the activity, suggested time needed for the activity, scale of the project, suggested group size, materials needed, resources for the activity, and how to prepare.

- **Implementation** This section of the activity provides the teacher with a step-by-step guide in implementing the activity, from its initial introduction to the students to the final presentation of the work product or class discussion. The Implementation section also ties the activity to its corresponding chapter in the textbook and ensures that students will have the requisite vocabulary to enhance their performance of the activity.

- **Assessment** Each activity provides the teacher with a variety of assessment suggestions that can be used to judge individual student and group performance of the activity.

- **Planning Guidelines and Project Task Sheet** Each activity provides a one-or two-page handout that can be given to students to explain the activity and their roles in it. These handouts provide a background for the activity, explain to students how to implement the activity, and describe the expectations for the final work product.

- **Standards for Evaluation** The final section of the activity provides the teacher with the criteria for evaluating individual or group performance as excellent, good, acceptable, or unacceptable. This page may be distributed to students to alert them to the standards against which their work on the activity will be judged.

Whether the activities are used in combination with teacher-directed lessons for the chapter, as a performance-based assessment of content mastery, or as an enrichment project, you may wish to debrief the class as a whole or in small groups at the close of each activity. Make sure that students understand the connection between the activity and the chapter content, and have them discuss how completing the activity has enhanced their understanding of American Government. You may also wish to give students the opportunity to practice their writing skills by having them write short reaction papers to selected activities in the booklet.

CHAPTER 1 ACTIVITY

A NEW GOVERNMENT FOR MARS

GOAL

In this activity students will learn about various forms of government by creating their own proposal for governing a hypothetical colony on Mars.

OVERVIEW

This project has five components: research, group discussion, proposal preparation, proposal presentation, and selection of the winning proposal. First, student groups each will research the principles, structure, officials, and laws of one of the following forms of government: monarchy, democratic republic, or dictatorship. Then group members will meet to discuss how they would structure a government for a hypothetical colony on Mars according to these principles. They will then prepare a written and/or oral presentation of their proposal. After all presentations have been made, the class will hold a discussion to decide which form of government would be most appropriate for the new colony on Mars.

OBJECTIVES

After completing this activity, students will be able to:
- explain the main principles of various forms of government;
- evaluate the functions of governments;
- discuss the relationship between government and the public good;
- analyze what is required to create a workable government.

LEARNING CONNECTIONS

- Learning Styles: interpersonal, linguistic, logical-mathematical
- Skills Mastery: acquiring information, defining problems, determining the strength of an argument; judging information, solving problems, synthesizing information
- *Connecting with Past Learning:* Chapter 1, Section 1—discussion of functions of govern-

ment and the public good; Chapter 1, Section 2—discussion of sources of authority

PLANNING

Purpose: You may use this activity in combination with teacher-directed lessons for this chapter, as a performance-based assessment of content mastery, or as an enrichment project.

Suggested Time: Plan to spend about five to seven 45-minute class periods on this project. Allow one class period to hold a class discussion about forms of government, introduce the activity, and organize groups. Give students one or two class periods to research their form of government. Allow at least one class period for students to prepare their presentations and another to present them. Limit presentations to about 10 to 15 minutes each, depending on the number of groups. You may need additional class periods to finish up the presentations and conduct a concluding discussion.

Scale of Project: Student groups can present their proposals at a long table in front of the class. Students will also need enough space to present a poster-sized chart of their form of government.

Group Size: Organize students into three groups. Each group will research and present one of the three forms of government discussed in the chapter. If you wish to have students work in smaller groups, organize students into six groups and have each pair of groups prepare and present competing proposals for their assigned form of government.

Materials: Students will need poster board and markers to prepare a chart of their government.

Resources: Have students use their textbooks, the Internet, the library, and any other materials that you provide to complete their research. Encourage students to explore and tap all available sources of information.

Preparation: Before starting the project, make copies of the Planning Guidelines and Task Sheet;

you will need at least one copy for each group. Each individual student should also receive a copy of the Criteria for Evaluation form that audience members will use to evaluate the project proposals. You may also wish to make copies of the Standards for Evaluation form—which is a project-specific rubric—for students to use in preparing their presentations.

IMPLEMENTATION

1. Introduce the activity by holding a class discussion on government. Ask students to describe the main functions of government and to discuss the relationship between government and the public good. Then make a list on the chalkboard of the major forms of government discussed in Chapter 1, and have students discuss how each carries out its functions.

2. Ensure that students understand the following terms: government, state, citizen, sovereignty, law, public policy, legitimacy, public good, monarchy, constitutional monarchy, republic, democracy, dictatorship, autocracy, oligarchy, authoritarian, totalitarian. If necessary, have students use the Glossary at the back of the textbook to write the definitions of these terms.

3. Assign or have students form into groups to represent the types of government discussed. Distribute copies of the Planning Guidelines and Task Sheet and, if you wish, copies of the Standards for Evaluation form. Have groups meet and discuss which functions their government will try to carry out. Then ask groups to assign individual or pairs of students to research their assigned government's principles, institutions, laws, and roles of government officials. Circulate among groups to make sure that students are on the right track.

4. Once students have completed their research, have students meet with their group to evaluate their findings. Have them compile their research into a proposal. Depending on time available, allow them to write a description or outline of their government or merely present their form of government in chart form. If time allows, students might prepare graphics or models of their government, including such

things as flags, logos, symbols of the new government, drawings, or a scale-model of a government building for their proposed colony.

5. Have students present their plan of government in front of the class. Have at least four students from each group present the proposal; each presenting his or her area researched: principles of government, institutions, laws, or roles of government leaders. Suggest that students play the role of a government official in charge of each area presented. Distribute the Criteria for Evaluation forms, which audience members can fill out during each presentation. Encourage audience members to ask questions or write down questions for later discussion.

6. After all groups have presented their proposals, hold a mock proposal-review meeting. Have students discuss the pros and cons of each form of government, evaluating how each of the proposals meets the criteria of the World Space Federation's Request for Proposal (RFP). Then ask the class to vote on which form of government would be best suited for the Mars colony. Encourage students to write a paragraph at the bottom of their Criteria for Evaluation forms summarizing their decisions.

ASSESSMENT

1. Use the Standards for Evaluation form to help you evaluate students during the presentation of proposals and on their written proposal.

2. Individual grades can be based on student evaluations of the proposals.

3. An option for additional individual assessment is to grade students' participation in the research stage of the activity by requesting a written summary of the research or individuals' contributions during the presentation.

4. Alternatively, you can assess student performance by using any or all of the following rubrics from the *Alternative Assessment Handbook* on the *One-Stop Planner CD-ROM:* Rubric 1: Acquiring Information, Rubric 7: Charts, Rubric 14: Group Activity, Rubric 24: Oral Presentations, Rubric 28: Posters, Rubric 30: Research.

PLANNING GUIDELINES

The World Space Federation (WSF) has announced plans for a daring new venture: the first human colony on Mars. With the discovery of water on the planet and the development of a device for building a breathable atmosphere, the "red planet" can now be colonized for human settlement. The WSF has issued a worldwide Request for Proposal (RFP) to any group willing to organize a government for the new colony. Each proposal must include a description of the government each group will establish on Mars. The written proposal should provide a summary of the form of government, its basic principles, its institutions, its laws, and the roles of its government officials. All proposals must be presented orally to the World Space Federation at their proposal-review meeting. The WSF will then decide which group is the most appropriate for pioneering a human settlement on Mars.

PROJECT TASK SHEET

Monarchy Group

As the ROYAL MARS SOCIETY, your assignment is to research and present a proposal for a monarchical form of government for the Mars colony.

Democratic Republic Group

As the UNITED MARS REPUBLIC, your assignment is to research and present a proposal for a democratic republic for the Mars colony.

Dictatorship Group

As the MAXIMUM POWER AUTHORITY, your assignment is to research and present a proposal for a dictatorship for the Mars colony.

A New Government for Mars

World Space Federation Proposal Review Meeting

CRITERIA FOR EVALUATION				
	Basic Principles of Government	Institutions	Laws	Roles of Government Leaders
Monarchy Group				
Democratic Republic Group				
Dictatorship Group				

Your Decision

Evaluate how well each group met each of the above criteria. On the basis of these criteria, which group would you choose to plant the first human settlement on Mars? Explain your reasoning below.

_____

_____

_____

_____

_____

_____

STANDARDS FOR EVALUATION

EXCELLENT

- The group meets all the RFP's criteria in an organized, thorough manner.
- The group's participation in the presentation shows that group members have fully researched their topics and have created a well-structured and workable government that matches its principles.
- All group members participate fully in the research and presentation of the proposal.

GOOD

- The group adequately meets all the RFP's criteria.
- The group's participation shows that group members have researched their assigned form of government adequately and have created a workable government that follows its principles.
- All group members participate in the research and presentation of the proposal.

ACCEPTABLE

- The group meets most of the RFP's criteria.
- The group's participation in the presentation shows that group members have researched most aspects of their assigned government and have created a rough plan of government that follows its principles.
- Most group members participate in the research and presentation of the proposal.

UNACCEPTABLE

- The group meets some of the RFP's criteria.
- The group's participation shows that group members have not researched their assigned government and have failed to create a government that follows its principles.
- Fewer than half of the group members participate in the research and presentation of the proposal.

COLONIAL UNION: WHAT'S YOUR OPINION?

GOAL

In this activity students will learn about the main attempts at uniting the separate colonial governments by creating a front page and an editorial page for a mock colonial newspaper.

OVERVIEW

This project has five components: group discussion; research; article and editorial writing, illustration creation, and political cartoon creation; layout of articles, illustrations, and political cartoons; and writing letters to the editor. First, student groups each will discuss the pros and cons of one of the plans to unite the American colonies, including the Albany Plan of Union, the Articles of Confederation, and the Constitution of the United States. Then group members will research the issue to prepare newspaper articles and accompanying illustrations about the attempt at union and editorials from several viewpoints along with political cartoons. Then group members will meet to lay out the articles, illustrations, editorials, and political cartoons in a mock colonial newspaper. They will then post the newspapers in a designated location so that students can read them and respond to the issues by writing a letter to the editor.

OBJECTIVES

After completing this activity, students will be able to:
- summarize several attempts at uniting colonial governments;
- identify the pros and cons of colonial unification;
- identify who supported and who opposed attempts at unification;
- evaluate arguments for and against colonial unification;
- write both informatively and expressively about topics in early American history;
- evaluate the power of the press;
- explain how political cartoons can be used to express a point of view;

- explain the nature and role of colonial newspapers in eighteenth-century America.

LEARNING CONNECTIONS

- Learning Styles: interpersonal, linguistic, logical-mathematical, visual-spatial
- Skills Mastery: acquiring information, creating political cartoons, determining the strength of an argument, distinguishing fact and opinion, judging information, making comparisons, recognizing point of view, synthesizing information, writing mastery: expressing, writing mastery: informing
- *Connecting with Past Learning:* Chapter 1, Section 1—discussion of functions of government and the public good; Chapter 2, Section 2—discussion of the search for colonial unity and the Albany Plan of Union; Chapter 2, Section 3—discussion of the Articles of Confederation; Chapter 2, Section 4—discussion of the Constitutional Convention and the U.S. Constitution; Chapter 2, Section 5—discussion of the debate over ratification of the U.S. Constitution

PLANNING

Purpose: You may use this activity in combination with teacher-directed lessons for this chapter, as a performance-based assessment of content mastery, or as an enrichment project.

Suggested Time: Plan to spend about five to seven 45-minute class periods on this project. Allow one class period to introduce the activity, organize groups, and hold group discussions about the assigned attempt at unification. Give students one or two class periods to research views both opposed to and favorable to unification. Also allow students one or two class periods to draft and finalize their articles and editorials and to sketch and finalize their illustrations and political cartoons. Then allow one class period for students to lay out and post their newspapers. You may need an additional class period to have students evaluate the newspapers and write a short letter to the editor.

Scale of Project: Student groups will need access to typewriters or computers to draft and finalize their articles and editorials. If these are unavailable, allow students to finalize their articles and editorials at home or to neatly hand-write them. Students also will need sufficient wall or hallway space to post their two-page newspapers.

Group Size: Organize students into three groups. Each group will research and prepare a two-page newspaper on one of the attempts at colonial unification discussed in the chapter. Direct the groups to designate some of their members as article writers, some as editorial writers, some as illustrators and layout people, and some as political cartoonists. All members of the group should participate in the research and discussion process and act as peer reviewers of each other's work. If you wish to have students work in smaller groups, organize students into six groups and have each pair of groups prepare and present competing newspapers covering their assigned attempt at colonial unification.

Materials: Students will need butcher paper or some other type of paper or poster board to lay out and present their articles and editorials. Illustrators and political cartoonists may need colored pencils or markers.

Resources: Have students use their textbooks, the Internet, the library, and any other materials that you provide to complete their research. In addition, students may wish to speak to the teacher-coordinator and/or members of the school newspaper to get tips and hints about how to prepare a newspaper. If feasible, students might also contact journalists, editors, and designers who work on your local newspaper. Encourage students to explore and tap all available sources of information.

Preparation: Before starting the project, make copies of the Planning Guidelines and Task Sheet; you will need at least one copy for each group. You may also wish to make copies of the Standards for Evaluation form—which is a project-specific rubric—for students to use in preparing their newspapers.

IMPLEMENTATION

1. Review with students the drive for independence among eighteenth-century Americans and the various plans for unification of the sep-arate colonial governments. Ask students to describe the Albany Plan of Union, the Articles of Confederation, and the U.S. Constitution, why they were developed, who their supporters and opponents were, and what was their outcome.

2. Ensure that students understand the following terms: constitution, rule of law, bicameral, Albany Plan of Union, tyranny, delegate, Articles of Confederation, ratification, Virginia Plan, New Jersey Plan, Great Compromise, Federalist, Antifederalist. If necessary, have students use the Glossary at the back of the textbook or a dictionary to write the definitions of these terms.

3. Assign or have students form into groups to represent the workers and publishers of a colonial newspaper. Distribute copies of the Planning Guidelines and Task Sheet and, if you wish, copies of the Standards for Evaluation form. Encourage groups to brainstorm about their assigned issue, identifying the reasons that people supported or opposed the attempt at unification. Then have students decide which position they will research. Circulate among the groups to help students identify the types of people who might represent different views. Have the groups designate who among their members will serve as article writers, editorial writers, illustrators, and political cartoonists.

4. Have groups use various sources to complete their research. Remind students to carefully note the sources of any direct quotations they might like to use in their articles and to use the direct quotations verbatim. Students also might want to look through library sources or on the Internet to find examples of what a colonial newspaper looked like.

5. Once students have completed their research, have each group write front-page articles summarizing the unification attempt and at least two editorials from the viewpoint of one of its supporters or critics. Remind the writers that their articles and editorials should be accompanied by informative yet succinct headlines. Each group should also prepare illustrations (perhaps sketches of individuals or colonial scenes) with accompanying captions for the front page and at least two political cartoons directed at the issue at hand for the editorial page.

6. Have students meet as a group to determine a name for their newspaper and to lay out their articles, illustrations, editorials, and political cartoons. Suggest that students design a masthead for the newspaper and also develop a slogan for the newspaper (something on the order of "All the news that's fit to print"). Remind students that their articles and illustrations should sit on the front page and that their editorials and political cartoons should sit on the editorial page. If students have the resources to create their own World Wide Web pages, have them post their newspapers so that other students can review them.

7. After all the groups have posted their newspapers on the designated wall or hallway space, have students read the articles, illustration captions, and editorials and examine the political cartoons. Then ask students to write a short letter to the editor of a newspaper produced by another group. The letter should express the student's opinions about the issues and the reasons for his or her views.

ASSESSMENT

1. Use the Standards for Evaluation form to help you evaluate students' articles, illustrations, editorials, cartoons, and letters to the editor.

2. Individual grades can be based on student articles, illustrations, editorials, and political cartoons.

3. An option for additional individual assessment is to grade students' letters to the editor.

4. Alternatively, you can assess student performance by using any or all of the following rubrics from the *Alternative Assessment Handbook* on the *One-Stop Planner CD-ROM:* Rubric 1: Acquiring Information, Rubric 3: Artwork, Rubric 12: Drawing Conclusions, Rubric 14: Group Activity, Rubric 16: Judging Information, Rubric 17: Letters to Editors, Rubric 23: Newspapers, Rubric 27: Political Cartoons, Rubric 30: Research, Rubric 41: Writing to Express, Rubric 42: Writing to Inform.

PLANNING GUIDELINES

The Boston *News-Letter* was the first permanent colonial newspaper. It began publication in 1704, and many other newspapers came into being in the decades that followed. Colonial newspapers thrived in the eighteenth century, printing information about politics and current events. Read the following excerpt from a colonial newspaper published on November 14, 1774. Use the writer's support of the Continental Congress as a guide in creating your own editorial in a mock colonial newspaper.

"On the Depravity of Kings and the Sovereignty of the People"

The American Congress derives [receives] all its power, wisdom, and justice, not from scrolls of parchment signed by kings but from the people. A more august [noble] and a more equitable [equal] legislative body never existed in any quarter of the globe. It is founded upon the principles of the most perfect liberty. A freeman, in honoring and obeying the Constitution, honors and obeys himself. The man who refuses to do both is a slave.

PROJECT TASK SHEET

Albany Plan of Union

Create a front page and an editorial page for a colonial newspaper for the year 1754. The front page should include articles about the Albany Plan of Union, including its purpose, structure, and principal supporters and critics. The front page should also include illustrations and accompanying captions. The editorial page should include views of supporters and critics of the union. Each editorial should be at least three paragraphs long. The editorial page should also include at least two political cartoons that express a point of view about the Albany Plan of Union.

Articles of Confederation

Create a front page and an editorial page for a colonial newspaper for the year 1777. The front page should include articles about the confederation, including its purpose, structure, and principal supporters and critics. The front page should also include illustrations and accompanying captions. The editorial page should include views of supporters and critics of the Articles of Confederation. Each editorial should be at least three paragraphs long. The editorial page should also include at least two political cartoons that express a point of view about the Articles of Confederation.

Constitution of the United States

Create a front page and an editorial page for a colonial newspaper for the year 1787. The front page should include articles about the Constitution, including its purpose, structure, and principal supporters and critics. The front page should also include illustrations and accompanying captions. The editorial page should include views of supporters and critics of the Constitution. Each editorial should be at least three paragraphs long. The editorial page should also include at least two political cartoons that express a point of view about the Constitution.

STANDARDS FOR EVALUATION

EXCELLENT

- The group's articles, headlines, and illustration captions provide a comprehensive and well-organized description of the unification attempt.
- The group's editorials and political cartoons thoroughly explore several viewpoints on the attempt at unification.
- All group members participate fully in the research, writing, illustration, and layout of the colonial newspaper.

GOOD

- The group's articles, headlines, and illustration captions provide a complete description of the unification attempt.
- The group's editorials and political cartoons present at least two viewpoints on the attempt at unification.
- All group members participate in the research, writing, illustration, and layout of the colonial newspaper.

ACCEPTABLE

- The group's articles, headlines, and illustration captions provide many of the major elements of the attempt at unification.
- The group's editorials and political cartoons present only two viewpoints on the attempt at unification.
- Most group members participate in the research, writing, illustration, and layout of the colonial newspaper.

UNACCEPTABLE

- The group's articles, headlines, and illustration captions provide only two or fewer of the issue's main elements.
- The group's editorials and political cartoons fail to present opposing viewpoints on the attempt at unification.
- Fewer than half of the group members participate in the research, writing, illustration, and layout of the colonial newspaper.

AMENDING THE CONSTITUTION: THE DOCUMENTARY

GOAL

In this activity students will learn about the main people, issues, and events behind the Constitution's amendments by producing a mock film documentary.

OVERVIEW

This project has four components: group discussion, research, script writing, and filming or presentation of the documentary. First, students will participate in a discussion about the constitutional amendment process. Then group members will research their segment of the documentary. Next, each group will write a script for one segment of the documentary. Students will then act out the roles of historical actors as they film or present their segments.

OBJECTIVES

After completing this activity, students will be able to:

- explain why the nation's founders established ways to amend the Constitution;
- summarize the steps in the constitutional amendment process;
- identify the main historical actors behind the Constitution's amendments;
- identify the historical events that influenced the passage of amendments;
- explain how the amendment process helps to make the Constitution a flexible document;
- discuss how amendments to the Constitution contribute to the public good.

LEARNING CONNECTIONS

- Learning Styles: body-kinesthetic, interpersonal, linguistic, logical-mathematical, visual-spatial
- Skills Mastery: acquiring information, recognizing point of view, synthesizing information, understanding cause and effect, writing mastery: creating, writing mastery: informing
- *Connecting with Past Learning:* Chapter 2, Section 4—discussion of the Constitutional Convention and the U.S. Constitution; Chapter 2, Section 5—discussion of the debate over a bill of rights; Chapter 3, Section 2—discussion of the constitutional amendment process and the 27 amendments

PLANNING

Purpose: You may use this activity in combination with teacher-directed lessons for this chapter, as a performance-based assessment of content mastery, or as an enrichment project.

Suggested Time: Plan to spend about 8 to 10 45-minute class periods on this project. Allow one class period to hold a group discussion about the amendment process, introduce the activity, and organize groups. Give students two or three class periods to research their assigned segment. Then allow two class periods for groups to write and coordinate their segments. Also allow three class periods for students to make costumes and sets and to film or present their segments. The director—either the teacher, a student, or group of students—may compile the segments into a finished movie either as a homework assignment or for extra credit. You may need an additional class period to have students view the documentary and evaluate it by writing movie reviews.

Scale of Project: You will need enough room for a television and videocassette recorder (VCR) in the front of the classroom. If students do not have access to the appropriate technology, they will need enough space to present their segments live or in the form of Hollywood-style storyboards in front of the class.

Group Size: Organize students into groups of three to five students. Each group will research, write a script for, and act out the roles of historical figures in one segment of a documentary on the Constitution's amendments. The members of each group should work cooperatively to fulfill all of their required tasks.

Materials: Groups will need a video camera to record their segments and a television and videocassette recorder to view their documentary. They may also need clothing for costumes and material to create sets. If video technology is not available, students may need poster board, markers, and other art supplies to create Hollywood-style storyboards—scenes drawn in cartoon format—of their documentary segment.

Resources: Have students use their textbooks, the Internet, the library, and any other materials that you provide to complete their research. If feasible, students might also contact history professors at universities or colleges in your community to discuss the history of the Constitution and its amendments. Encourage students to explore and tap all available sources of information.

Preparation: Before starting the project, make copies of the Planning Guidelines and Project Task Sheet; you will need at least one copy for each group. You may also wish to make copies of the Standards for Evaluation form—which is a project-specific rubric—for students to use in preparing their documentary segments.

IMPLEMENTATION

1. Give students an overview of the activity by describing its four stages. Tell students that they will discuss the amendment process before researching a particular amendment. They will then work with their groups to research the people, issues, and events behind a particular amendment. After they write a script for a segment of a documentary on their amendment, they will then film, act out, or present their segments of the documentary on storyboards.

2. To begin a discussion of the amendment process, have students review the "Citizenship in Action" feature on the Twenty-seventh Amendment, which appears on textbook page 54. Ask students to identify the main people behind the amendment. *(James Madison, Gregory Watson)* Draw a time line on the chalkboard, beginning with 1789 and ending with 1992. Have students fill in the major events that led to the ratification of the amendment. *(1789: Amendment first introduced; Maryland ratifies amendment. 1982: Watson begins campaign. 1991: Senate votes on a pay raise. 1992: Michigan becomes 38th, and final, state to ratify amendment)* Ask students to identify the two ratification methods used to approve an amendment and identify which one was used to pass the Twenty-seventh amendment. *(approval*

by three fourths of the state legislatures) Then have students identify the main tactic Watson used to get state legislatures' approval. *(letters to state legislators)*

3. Ensure that students understand the following terms: amendment, propose, ratify, repeal, Bill of Rights, and Article V. It might be helpful to list terms on the chalkboard and have students define the terms. Alternatively, you might hand out copies of the Planning Guidelines and ask a volunteer to read aloud Article V of the Constitution, which is printed there. Students might analyze the use of some of the key terms in the article. If necessary, have students use the Glossary at the back of the textbook to write the definitions of these terms.

4. Organize the class into groups of three to five students. Distribute copies of the Planning Guidelines and Project Task Sheet and, if you wish, copies of the Standards for Evaluation form. Go over the instructions on the Planning Guidelines to make sure that students understand the assignment. Either assign or have each group choose an amendment from the list on the Project Task Sheet. If the groups choose their own amendments, act as the documentary's director and circulate among the class to make sure that there is no overlap. If students would like to focus the documentary on one particular issue, such as voting rights, have groups choose their amendments only from that category.

5. Have student groups begin researching their segments. Groups might assign members to serve as actors, costume/set designers, or writers to help divide up the research. In addition to reading histories of their particular amendment, encourage students to look for historical speeches, biographies of key people, and historical-costume books to help recreate the key people and scenes involved in their particular amendment.

6. Once students have completed their research, have each group meet in a "story meeting" to discuss how to turn their research into a narrative, or story. Groups might first create a time line to identify key events in the amendment proposal and ratification process. Using this time line, groups should write a script with scenes that describe the people, events, and issues behind their amendment. Have students use the script to present their documentary

segment—either filmed, acted out, or in the form of storyboards—to the class. If possible, have either the teacher or student volunteers compile and edit the filmed segments into a completed documentary.

7. After the documentary segments have been presented, have students view the completed film (if available) and discuss the key people and events of the amendment and ratification process in each segment. Then ask students to write a short movie review of the documentary. The reviews should summarize and evaluate how each amendment was ratified, the main people who helped ratify it, and the events or issues that triggered the amendment proposal. Movie reviews should also evaluate the structure and effectiveness of each segment in presenting the amendment process.

ASSESSMENT

1. Use the Standards for Evaluation form to help you evaluate students' work in creating their documentary segments.

2. Individual grades can be based on student participation in research, writing, set and costume design, or presentation of the documentary segment.

3. An option for additional individual assessment is to grade students' movie reviews.

4. Alternatively, you can assess student performance by using any or all of the following rubrics from the *Alternative Assessment Handbook* on the *One-Stop Planner CD-ROM:* Rubric 1: Acquiring Information, Rubric 3: Artwork, Rubric 4: Biographies, Rubric 6: Cause and Effect, Rubric 14: Group Activity, Rubric 22: Multimedia Presentations, Rubric 30: Research, Rubric 33: Skits and Reader's Theater, Rubric 39: Writing to Create, Rubric 42: Writing to Inform.

PLANNING GUIDELINES

"The Congress, whenever two thirds of both houses shall deem it necessary, shall propose amendments to this Constitution, or, on the application of the legislatures of two thirds of the several states, shall call a convention for proposing amendments, which, in either case, shall be valid to all intents and purposes, as part of this Constitution, when ratified by the legislatures of three fourths of the several states, or by conventions in three fourths thereof, as the one or the other mode of ratification may be proposed by the Congress; provided that no amendment which may be made prior to the year one thousand eight hundred and eight shall in any manner affect the first and fourth clauses in the ninth section of the first article; and that no state, without its consent, shall be deprived of its equal suffrage in the Senate."

—Article V of the U.S. Constitution

A Dynamic Documentary: The People who Amended the Constitution

Director D.W. Douglass is planning to film a documentary on the amendments to the U.S. Constitution. Douglass wants to bring the amendments to life by presenting them in the voices of the people who helped get them ratified. As part of a production group, your assignment is to research, write, and create one of the segments of the documentary. You will research the people, main events, and issues behind the passage of a particular amendment. Then your group will write a script, create costumes and sets, and play the roles of key people—using actual speeches when possible—for your segment.

PROJECT TASK SHEET

Civil Rights
* **The Thirteenth Amendment:** Abolished slavery; ratified in 1865.
* **The Fourteenth Amendment:** Equal Protection Clause; ratified in 1868.
* **The Fifteenth Amendment:** Voting for African American males; ratified in 1870.

Voting Rights
* **The Fifteenth Amendment**: Voting for African American males; ratified in 1870.
* **The Nineteenth Amendment:** Voting for women; ratified in 1920.
* **The Twenty-third Amendment:** Voting in Washington, D.C.; ratified in 1961.
* **The Twenty-fourth Amendment:** Abolished poll tax; ratified in 1964.
* **The Twenty-sixth Amendment:** Voting for 18-year-olds; ratified in 1971.

Elected Officials
* **The Twelfth Amendment:** Election of the president and vice president; ratified in 1804.
* **The Seventeenth Amendment:** Electing senators; ratified in 1913.
* **The Twentieth Amendment:** President's term and succession; ratified in 1933.
* **The Twenty-second Amendment:** Two-term limit for president; ratified in 1951.
* **The Twenty-fifth Amendment:** Presidential succession; ratified in 1967.

STANDARDS FOR EVALUATION

EXCELLENT

- The group's segment provides a comprehensive and well-organized description of the issues and events of the amendment process.
- The group's segment thoroughly explores the views of more than two people who helped ratify the amendment.
- All group members participate fully in the research, writing, and acting of the segment.

GOOD

- The group's segment provides a complete description of the issues and events of the amendment process.
- The group's segment presents at least two people who helped ratify the amendment.
- All group members participate in the research, writing, and acting of the segment.

ACCEPTABLE

- The group's segment provides many of the major events of the amendment process.
- The group's segment presents only one person who helped ratify the amendment.
- Most group members participate in the research, writing, and acting of the segment.

UNACCEPTABLE

- The group's segment provides only two or fewer of the events of the amendment process.
- The group's segment fails to present any of the people involved in the amendment process.
- Fewer than half of the group members participate in the research, writing, and acting of the segment.

GOVERNMENT POWERS: HEADLINE HUNT

GOAL

In this activity students will learn about federal, state, and shared government powers by identifying them in the headlines of newspapers and newsmagazines.

OVERVIEW

This project has three components: group discussion, "The Power of Headlines" worksheet, and a "Headline Hunt." First, students will participate in a discussion about the powers assigned to the federal and state governments and the powers denied to both levels of government. Then students will identify these powers in mock headlines. Next, individual students will find headlines of their own that give examples of federal, state, and shared government powers.

OBJECTIVES

After completing this activity, students will be able to:

- identify powers given to the federal government;
- identify powers reserved to state governments;
- identify powers shared by both federal and state governments;
- distinguish between powers given to government and those denied to government;
- analyze the content of news headlines;
- provide real-world examples of government powers.

LEARNING CONNECTIONS

- Learning Styles: intrapersonal; linguistic, logical-mathematical; visual-spatial
- Skills Mastery: acquiring information, classifying information; drawing conclusions, judging information, making comparisons, synthesizing information
- ***Connecting with Past Learning:*** Chapter 2, Section 4—discussion of rival constitutional plans; Chapter 2, Section 5—discussion of strong versus weak central government; Chapter 3, Section 1—discussion of federalism; Chapter 3, Section 2—discussion of Tenth Amendment; Chapter 4, Section 1—discussion of federal and state powers

PLANNING

Purpose: You may use this activity in combination with teacher-directed lessons for this chapter, as a performance-based assessment of content mastery, or as an enrichment project.

Suggested Time: Plan to spend about two or three 45-minute class periods on this project. Allow one class period to hold a group discussion about government powers, introduce the activity, and have students complete the "The Power of Headlines" worksheet. Give students another class period to conduct the "Headline Hunt," or assign it as homework. You may want to take additional time to allow students to create a collage of their headlines.

Scale of Project: Students may need wall or hallway space to hang posters of their collages.

Group Size: Students should complete the worksheet and "Headline Hunt" individually. Students may work together to create optional collages.

Materials: Students may need poster board, glue, and scissors if they create poster collages of their headlines.

Resources: Have students use the textbook to complete "The Power of Headlines" worksheet and use discarded newspapers and newsmagazines to complete the "Headline Hunt."

Preparation: Before starting the project, make copies of the "The Power of Headlines" worksheet and "Headline Hunt" Project Task Sheet; you will need one copy for each student. You may also wish to make copies of the Standards for Evaluation form—which is a project-specific rubric—for students to use in completing the activity.

IMPLEMENTATION

1. Give students an overview of the activity by describing its three stages. Tell students that they will discuss three types of government

powers: those given to the federal government, those reserved to the states, and those shared by both the federal and state governments (concurrent powers). They also will discuss powers denied to both levels of government. They will then complete a worksheet activity, called "The Power of Headlines," to identify government powers. Next, they will use discarded newspapers or newsmagazines to find three headlines of their own that give examples of federal, state, and concurrent powers.

2. To begin a discussion of government powers, write these three headings on the chalkboard: *Federal Government Powers, State Government Powers, Shared Powers.* Then have students provide real-life examples for each heading, and write the examples on the chalkboard under the appropriate heading. Students may need to refer to the "Government Powers" chart on textbook page 69 for additional help.

3. Ensure that students understand the following terms: expressed power, implied power, elastic clause, inherent power, reserved power, concurrent power. Ask volunteers to define the terms and identify which of them correspond to the examples written on the chalkboard. If necessary, have students use the Glossary at the back of the textbook to write the definitions of these terms.

4. Distribute copies of "The Power of Headlines" worksheet. Go over the instructions to make sure that students understand the assignment.

5. After students have completed the worksheets, review with them the instructions for the Project Task Sheet "Headline Hunt." If you wish,

distribute copies of the Standards for Evaluation form.

6. Once students have completed the "Headline Hunt," have them turn in their work. After you have graded the assignments, return them to the students. As an optional activity, have students create three collages of the headlines on poster boards, one for federal government powers, one for state powers, and one for shared powers.

7. Have students hang their optional collages in a designated area of the classroom or hallway so that their classmates may examine them. Use the time to clarify any confusion students may have about federalism.

ASSESSMENT

1. Use the Standards for Evaluation form to help you evaluate student headlines.

2. Individual grades can be based on "The Power of Headlines" worksheet and the "Headline Hunt" activity.

3. Alternatively, you can assess student performance by using any or all of the following rubrics from the *Alternative Assessment Handbook* on the *One-Stop Planner CD-ROM:* Rubric 8: Collages, Rubric 9: Comparing and Contrasting; Rubric 12: Drawing Conclusions, Rubric 16: Judging Information, Rubric 28: Posters.

THE POWER OF HEADLINES

Although we often take them for granted, government powers make headlines every day. Below, you will find mock headlines that summarize some of these important government powers. Read each headline. In the first blank, write the government power reflected in the headline. (*Hint:* Use the chart on textbook page 69 for a list of these powers.) Then fill in the second blank with one of the following letters to identify which level of government the power is assigned to. An example is given below.

    a. federal power   **c.** shared (concurrent) power
    b. state (reserved) power   **d.** denied power

Example:

conduct elections	b	Record Number of Ballots Printed for Upcoming Election
1. _____	__	Record Debt Saddles Government with Heavy Payments
2. _____	__	New Design for $100 Bill Thwarts Counterfeiters
3. _____	__	Polling Places to Increase by 10% This Election
4. _____	__	On the Bench: New Court to Open in Former Gymnasium
5. _____	__	Officials Set Tougher Medical Licensing
6. _____	__	Military Spending Increase Approved
7. _____	__	More Immigration Agents to Police Borders
8. _____	__	Stricter Regulations for Water Quality Pass Legislature
9. _____	__	New Interstate Highway Proposed
10. _____	__	Scientist Knighted By U.S. For Anti-Cancer Efforts
11. _____	__	War Looms Between U.S. and Iraq
12. _____	__	Public Schools to Get New Computers
13. _____	__	Tax Revenues Up for Third Straight Year
14. _____	__	Marriage Licenses Now Made Simpler
15. _____	__	Puerto Rico Gets New Government Building
16. _____	__	NAFTA's Gains and Losses for U.S. Businesses
17. _____	__	Record Number of Women-Owned Businesses Incorporated
18. _____	__	Massachusetts Prints First State Currency
19. _____	__	Voter Registration Materials Available Tomorrow
20. _____	__	Bank Charters Decline As Mergers Increase

PROJECT TASK SHEET

HEADLINE HUNT

Using discarded newspapers or newsmagazines, find headlines of your own that relate to government powers. Find at least one that corresponds to a federal power, one for a state (reserved) power, and one for a shared (concurrent) power. Photocopy the headline, newspaper or newsmagazine title, and the date for each. Paste each headline and supporting information on a sheet of paper, and identify the type of power and level of government each headline matches.

STANDARDS FOR EVALUATION

EXCELLENT

- The student provides more than one headline for each of the following categories: federal government power, state government power, and shared (concurrent) power.
- The student correctly identifies the type of power and level of government for all of the headlines.

GOOD

- The student provides at least one headline for each of the following categories: federal government power, state government power, and shared (concurrent) power.
- The student correctly identifies the type of power and level of government for all of the headlines.

ACCEPTABLE

- The student provides one headline for each of the following categories: federal government power, state government power, and shared (concurrent) power.
- The student correctly identifies the types of power and levels of government for most of the headlines.

UNACCEPTABLE

- The student does not provide a headline for all of the following categories: federal government power, state government power, and shared (concurrent) power.
- The student does not correctly identify the types of power and levels of government for the headlines.

ANSWERS TO "THE POWER OF HEADLINES" WORKSHEET

1. borrow money; c
2. print money; a
3. conduct elections; b
4. establish courts; c
5. license professionals; b
6. support armed forces; a
7. regulate immigration; a
8. make laws; c
9. establish roads; a
10. denied power; d
11. declare war; a
12. support public schools; b
13. collect taxes; c
14. make marriage laws; b
15. govern U.S. territories; a
16. regulate foreign trade; a
17. incorporate business firms; b
18. denied power; d
19. determine voter qualifications; b
20. charter banks; a

STATE CONGRESSIONAL DISTRICT: MAP IT!

GOAL

In this activity students will learn about the boundaries, demographics, and representatives of their state congressional districts by creating a map of their state districts.

OVERVIEW

This project has three components: group discussion, research, and creation of the map. First, students will participate in a discussion about congressional districts. Then student groups will research the boundaries, demographics, and representative of each congressional district in their state. Next, the groups will compile their research findings and create a wall-sized map of their state's congressional districts.

OBJECTIVES

After completing this activity, students will be able to:

- explain why the states are divided into congressional districts;
- explain the relationship between the decennial census and the determination of congressional districts;
- discuss how state districts are represented in Congress;
- describe controversies that have arisen over the drawing of congressional district boundaries;
- identify their state's congressional districts;
- describe the demographics of their state's congressional districts;
- identify their state's congressional representatives;
- compare and contrast characteristics of their state's congressional districts;
- compile statistics in graphs and/or charts;
- create a map;
- present numerical information in a map.

LEARNING CONNECTIONS

- Learning Styles: body-kinesthetic, interpersonal, logical-mathematical, visual-spatial

- Skills Mastery: acquiring information, creating maps, making comparisons, navigating the Internet, presenting data graphically, synthesizing information
- ***Connecting with Past Learning:*** Chapter 5, Section 2—discussion of the U.S. House of Representatives

PLANNING

Purpose: You may use this activity in combination with teacher-directed lessons for this chapter, as a performance-based assessment of content mastery, or as an enrichment project.

Suggested Time: Plan to spend about four to six 45-minute class periods on this project. Allow one class period to hold a group discussion about state congressional districts, introduce the activity, and organize groups. Give students one or two class periods to conduct research on their assigned congressional district. Then allow one or two class periods for the student groups to compile their collected information on a large wall map. You may need an additional class period to have students evaluate and compare the demographics of the various state congressional districts.

Scale of Project: You will need enough room for students to put together map information and enough wall or hallway space to display the final state congressional district map.

Group Size: Group size will depend on the number of students in your class and the number of congressional districts in your state. For states with a large number of congressional districts, individual students can research the main features of each congressional district. For states with fewer congressional districts, groups can research more detailed statistics.

Materials: Students will need a large poster board or butcher-block paper or other appropriate type of paper, map pencils and markers, and scissors and glue to produce the final map. Students may also need graph paper.

Resources: Have students use their textbooks, the Internet, the library, and any other materials that you provide to complete their research. The U.S. Bureau of the Census, and particularly its World Wide Web site (http://www.ccnsus. gov/datamap/www/), has a compilation of demographic information organized by congressional district. If feasible, students may wish to contact geography professors at universities or colleges in your community to learn more about how statistical and demographic information may be displayed on a map. Similarly, students may wish to contact professional cartographers working in your community. Encourage students to explore and tap all available sources of information.

Preparation: Before starting the project, make copies of the Planning Guidelines and Project Task Sheet; you will need one copy for each student. You may also wish to make copies of the Standards for Evaluation form—which is a project-specific rubric—for students to use in preparing their maps. You should also determine the number of congressional districts in your state before you begin the project.

IMPLEMENTATION

1. Give students an overview of the activity by describing its three stages. Tell students that they will first discuss the process of setting the number and location of congressional districts in each state. Next they will work in groups (or individually, as discussed earlier) to research the boundaries, demographics, and representatives of the congressional districts in their state. They will then compile all of the collected information and combine it to create a large state map showing their state's congressional districts and the demographic features of the various congressional districts.

2. Begin the discussion of state congressional districts by asking students to name their representative in the House of Representatives and to identify their congressional district. If students do not know the answers to these questions, guide them in determining how they might find out this information. Then ask students to recall from the textbook discussion how a state's congressional districts are established. *(Taken every 10 years, the census determines how many of the 435 seats in the House of Representatives are allotted to each state;*

each state then establishes that number of congressional districts.) Have students discuss what controversies have arisen over the drawing of congressional district boundaries. *(lower population in different districts; gerrymandering; racial balance of districts)*

3. Ensure that students understand the following terms: census, apportion, gerrymandering. If necessary, have students use the Glossary at the back of the textbook to write the definitions of these terms.

4. Assign or have students form into groups according to the number of congressional districts in your state (or assign or have individual students choose individual congressional districts). Distribute copies of the Planning Guidelines and Project Task Sheet to the students and, if you wish, copies of the Standards for Evaluation form. Go over the instructions to make sure that students understand the assignment. Also make sure that each group or student knows which congressional district to research.

5. Have student groups begin researching the characteristics of their respective congressional districts. Groups might assign members to research a particular characteristic, such as the district's boundaries, facts about the representative, population, gender and racial makeup of the population, or voting-age population. Encourage students to come up with as complete a statistical snapshot as they can to describe their district. Students might present this information in the form of graphs, charts, tables, or illustrations.

6. Once students have completed their research, have the class meet as a group to create the final map. Have a volunteer create a wall-sized outline of the state on a large poster board or butcher-block paper. Then have each group fill in the boundaries of its congressional district and label it. Groups should then fill in their respective congressional districts with the demographic information, graphic illustrations, and pictures they have compiled.

7. After students have completed the final map, have the groups or individual students present an overview of their congressional districts. Ask students to compare and contrast the demographics of the congressional districts, including their population and racial or ethnic makeup. You might also ask students to discuss

whether the people of the state are fairly represented under the current organization of congressional districts. Alternatively, have students write a short paragraph or brief essay in response to the same question.

ASSESSMENT

1. Use the Standards for Evaluation form to help you evaluate students' work in creating their contribution to the state congressional district map.

2. Individual grades can be based on student participation in researching or presenting information on the map.

3. An option for additional individual assessment is to grade students' paragraphs or essays.

4. Alternatively, you can assess student performance by using any or all of the following rubrics from the *Alternative Assessment Handbook* on the *One-Stop Planner CD-ROM:* Rubric 1: Acquiring Information, Rubric 3: Artwork, Rubric 7: Charts, Rubric 9: Comparing and Contrasting, Rubric 11: Discussions, Rubric 14: Group Activity, Rubric 20: Map Creation, Rubric 30: Research, Rubric 41: Writing to Express.

PLANNING GUIDELINES

You and your classmates will create a wall-sized map of your state congressional districts. Each congressional district will be illustrated with population statistics and information about the district's representative. This map will provide you with an overall picture of congressional representation in your state.

PROJECT TASK SHEET

Your assignment is to describe the geography and demographics of Congressional District _____. Use the checklist below to help you find information about your district. You will then compile the information in a state map. Be sure to think carefully about the best way to present the information. For example, you may wish to use tables, bar graphs, pie charts, and pictures to present statistics and other information.

- Boundaries of congressional district (photocopy source)

- Congressional district representative (locate photograph and biographical information)

- Major cities in congressional district _____

- Location(s) of representative's offices in district _____

- 2000 census population of district _____

- Ethnic/racial breakdown of population _____

- Number of men and women _____

- Number of voting-age people and their percentage of total population _____

- Number of elementary schools/middle schools/high schools _____

- Number of colleges and universities _____

- Major agricultural products _____

- Additional statistics: _____

_____

_____

_____

_____

_____

_____

_____

_____

_____

STANDARDS FOR EVALUATION

EXCELLENT

- The group or individual student presents accurate geographic boundaries, complete information about the district's representative, and a detailed statistical portrait of the congressional district.
- The group's or individual student's congressional district map presents information in a neat, organized, and compelling format.
- All group members (or individual student) participate fully in the research and illustration of the congressional district map.

GOOD

- The group or individual student presents accurate geographic boundaries, information about the district's representative, and at least four statistics about the congressional district.
- The group's or individual student's congressional district map presents information in a neat and organized format.
- All group members (or individual student) participate fully in the research and illustration of the congressional district map.

ACCEPTABLE

- The group or individual student presents accurate geographic boundaries, some information about the district's representative, and at least two statistics about the congressional district.
- The group's or individual student's congressional district map presents information in an organized format.
- Most group members (or individual student) participate fully in the research and illustration of the congressional district map.

UNACCEPTABLE

- The group or individual student presents inaccurate geographic boundaries, little information about the district's representative, and few statistics about the congressional district.
- The group's or individual student's congressional district map presents information in a disorganized format.
- Few group members participate fully in the research and illustration of the congressional district map.

IT'S YOUR GOVERNMENT—MAKE A LAW

GOAL

In this activity students will learn about the key events in the legislative process by preparing and debating a hypothetical bill.

OVERVIEW

This project has seven components: group discussion of the legislative process, research, preparation of a hypothetical bill, writing of testimony and questions, committee hearings, preparation of committee report, and floor consideration. First, students will participate in a discussion about the key steps in making a law. Then students will research their assigned roles in the lawmaking process. One student group will prepare a bill for consideration. Next, students will prepare testimony and questions for the committee hearing. Students will next hold a mock committee hearing, then prepare a committee report on the hearing. Finally, the entire class will debate the bill and vote whether or not to pass it.

OBJECTIVES

After completing this activity, students will be able to:
- identify the main steps in the legislative process;
- describe how a bill is prepared;
- identify the kinds of committees there are in Congress;
- explain the workings of the congressional committee system;
- explain how bills are referred to committees;
- discuss the purpose of congressional committee hearings;
- prepare and analyze testimony in support of or in opposition to a bill;
- analyze views for and against an idea;
- debate important issues;
- determine whether or not a bill promotes the public good.

LEARNING CONNECTIONS

- *Learning Styles:* interpersonal, linguistic, logical-mathematical
- *Skills Mastery:* acquiring information, defining problems, determining the strength of an argument, distinguishing fact and opinion, drawing conclusions, judging information, navigating the Internet, recognizing points of view, synthesizing information, writing mastery: describing, writing mastery: persuading
- *Connecting with Past Learning:* Chapter 1, Section 1—discussion of functions of government and discussion of the public good; Chapter 5, Section 1—discussion of the role of Congress; Chapter 6, Section 2—discussion of the congressional committee system; Chapter 6, Section 3—discussion of the legislative process

PLANNING

Purpose: You may use this activity in combination with teacher-directed lessons for this chapter, as a performance-based assessment of content mastery, or as an enrichment project.

Suggested Time: Plan to spend about eight to ten 45-minute class periods on this project. Allow one class period to hold a group discussion about the legislative process, introduce the activity, and assign roles. Give students two or three class periods to research their assigned roles and prepare written materials. Then allow one or two class periods for students to hold committee hearings. Next, give students two class periods to prepare the committee report. Once the report is finished, allow students to read the report and then take one class period for floor debate. You may need an additional class period to identify the additional steps needed to make the bill a law.

Scale of Project: You will need enough room for students to set up chairs in front of the class for the committee hearings. If insufficient space

HRW material copyrighted under notice appearing earlier in this work.

is available, you may wish to reserve a larger area in the school such as a meeting room, cafeteria, or auditorium.

Group Size: For the most part, you will assign roles to individual students. However, if you wish, you can create two groups of at least four people: (1) a group to prepare the bill and (2) a group to serve as the committee staff.

Materials: Students may need a tape recorder or video camera to help in making a transcript of the committee hearings.

Resources: Have students use their textbooks, the Internet, the library, and any other materials that you provide to complete their research. Inform the students that the U.S. House of Representatives World Wide Web site (http://www.house.gov/) provides detailed information about the legislative process, including committees, rules, procedures, processes, and examples of public hearings testimony. Encourage students to explore and tap all available sources of information.

Preparation: Before starting the project, make copies of the Planning Guidelines and Project Task Sheet; you will need one copy for each student. You may also wish to make copies of the Standards for Evaluation form—which is a project-specific rubric—for students to use in preparing their assigned roles.

IMPLEMENTATION

1. Give students an overview of the activity by describing its seven stages. Tell students that they will first discuss the steps involved in the legislative process. They will then research assigned roles they will play in the lawmaking process. One group will prepare a bill for legislative consideration, and others will take on the roles of committee members and witnesses as they prepare and hold a committee hearing. Next, one group will act as committee staff members to prepare the hearing report. Finally, the entire class will debate and vote on the bill.

2. Before you begin the class discussion of the legislative process, draw on the chalkboard a simple flowchart containing seven boxes. In the first box, write "Bill is introduced." Then ask students to list the remaining steps needed to turn the bill into a law. Write the students' responses in the appropriate boxes. *(referral to committee, hearings, markup, floor considera-*

tion, conference committee, presidential action) Ask a volunteer to come to the chalkboard and draw in the needed directional arrows. You may wish to refer any students who need help to the Chapter 6 Summary.

3. Ensure that students understand the following terms: bill, committee, hearing, markup, floor consideration, filibuster. If necessary, have students use the Glossary at the back of the textbook to write the definitions of these terms, or have them discern the definitions in the context of the textbook discussion.

4. Distribute copies of the Planning Guidelines and Project Task Sheet to each student. Go over the instructions with the class to make sure that students understand the assignment. Act as Speaker of the House and either assign or help coordinate as students choose a role to play in the simulation. If you wish, distribute copies of the Standards for Evaluation form.

5. Have students begin researching their assigned roles. Refer them to the House of Representatives World Wide Web site if they have access to the Internet. Ask the group writing the bill to make the text available to other students to help them prepare their testimony.

6. Once students have completed their research and the bill is written, have students prepare their written materials. Students acting as witnesses should prepare written statements of their testimony, which should be given to the members of the committee before the hearing begins. Students acting as committee members should use the testimony to prepare a list of questions for each of the witnesses.

7. After students have completed their written materials, have the committee hold the hearings. You may wish to help the committee chair organize and run the hearings. The committee chair should make sure that witness testimonies last no longer than five minutes. Also, the chair should limit committee members' questions to five minutes. The official reporter(s) should record both the testimony and the questions. After the hearing has reached an end, have the recorder prepare an official transcript of the hearing proceedings.

8. Using the official transcript, the group acting as committee staff members should meet to prepare a committee report that details the purpose and scope of the proposed bill, any

amendments that need to be added to the bill, an estimate of the cost involved in implementing the bill, and the powers granted to Congress that allow them to prepare this bill. The group should then make the final report available for class members to read.

9. Once students have read the report, hold a mock debate on the House floor to vote on the bill. Allow students to add amendments to the bill. Have them take a final vote and decide whether or not the bill should continue on to the Senate. Ask students to explain what additional steps are needed before the bill can become a law. *(bill must be approved by the Senate; conference committee must meet to approve any changes in the bill; president must sign the bill into law)*

ASSESSMENT

1. Use the Standards for Evaluation form to help you evaluate student participation in the simulation.

2. Individual grades can be based on written materials produced during the simulation.

3. An option for additional individual assessment is to grade students' participation in the floor debate.

4. Alternatively, you can assess student performance by using any or all of the following rubrics from the *Alternative Assessment Handbook* on the *One-Stop Planner CD-ROM:* Rubric 1: Acquiring Information, Rubric 10: Debates, Rubric 11: Discussions, Rubric 12: Drawing Conclusions, Rubric 14: Group Activity, Rubric 16: Judging Information, Rubric 30: Research, Rubric 35: Solving Problems, Rubric 40: Writing to Describe, Rubric 43: Writing to Persuade.

PLANNING GUIDELINES

Just south of the growing city of Ferndale, a wilderness thick with trees and wildlife spreads across more than 5,000 acres. A river runs through the wilderness, providing water for the city. The red-eared fern, the only kind like it in the world, grows abundantly in the woods. Two endangered animals, including the purple grouse and the blue fox, also make their home there. Thousands of hikers, campers, students on field trips, and off-road bicyclists enjoy the public areas of this wilderness.

However, the Homestead Corporation, which owns nearly half of this wilderness area, has just announced its plans to build a new residential subdivision in the wilderness. Thousands of acres of trees will be cut down to make room for houses and apartment buildings, including units for senior citizens and low-income families.

Concerned residents, environmentalists, and recreational enthusiasts have joined together to keep the company from building on and developing its land. The congressperson from the district has decided to sponsor a congressional bill to declare the area a National Wilderness protected by the federal government.

Your assignment is to decide whether this bill should become law. Class members will write the bill, hold committee hearings to explore the effects of the bill from both sides of the issue, and debate the bill on the House floor. The Project Task Sheet lists the roles needed to conduct the simulation.

PROJECT TASK SHEET

- **Congresspeople** (4 to 6): Prepare written text of bill
- **Official Reporter** (1 or 2): Record testimony at committee hearing and provide official transcript of hearing for the class
- **Committee on Resources Members** (4 to 6): Prepare questions for witnesses at hearing
- **Committee on Resources Chairperson:** Announce date, place, and subject of hearing; make a brief introductory statement to begin hearing; read bill aloud; call witnesses; limit testimony and questions to five minutes
- **Witnesses:** Provide written and oral testimony for the Committee on Resources
- **Owner of Homestead Corporation**
- **Representative from local Chamber of Commerce**
- **Representative from Nature Club, an environmental group**

- **Representative from Free Wheelers, an off-road bicycling club**
- **National Park ranger**
- **Biology professors who have studied the red-eared fern, the purple grouse, and the blue fox**
- **Representative of homeowners association near wilderness area**
- **Representative of housing group for low-income and retired people**
- **Students from local schools**
- **Congressperson representing district**
- **Staff Members of Committee on Resources** (4 to 6): Prepare a written report on the bill after the hearing, which includes purpose and scope of the bill, any amendments that need to be added, an estimate of the cost of implementing the bill, and the powers granted to Congress that allow them to prepare this bill

STANDARDS FOR EVALUATION

EXCELLENT

- Student demonstrates a thorough knowledge of the responsibilities of his or her assigned role.
- Student performs his or her assigned duties competently, creatively, and collaboratively.
- Student's written information is well researched and presented in an organized, complete format.

GOOD

- Student demonstrates a complete knowledge of the responsibilities of his or her assigned role.
- Student performs his or her assigned duties competently and collaboratively.
- Student's written information is well researched and presented in an organized, complete format.

ACCEPTABLE

- Student demonstrates a basic knowledge of the responsibilities of his or her assigned role.
- Student performs his or her assigned duties competently.
- Student's written information is adequately researched and presented.

UNACCEPTABLE

- Student demonstrates a lack of knowledge of the responsibilities of his or her assigned role.
- Student fails to perform his or her assigned duties.
- Student fails to provide written information for this project.

DEAR PRESIDENT: ADVICE TO THE OVAL OFFICE

GOAL

In this activity students will learn about the various roles of the president of the United States by writing a mock letter from the president and preparing an advice column.

OVERVIEW

This project has five components: group discussion, research, letter writing, drafting an advice column, and presentation of advice columns. First, students will participate in a discussion of the roles and responsibilities of the president of the United States. Student groups will then research the various roles of the president through the use of newspapers, magazine articles, and the Internet. Next, student groups will draft and discuss a letter from the president to an advice columnist requesting help in prioritizing these responsibilities. Group members will then adopt the role of advice columnists and respond to the president's letter. Each group will present its advice column to the class, and the class will vote in order to determine which advice column most effectively helps the president balance the often-conflicting roles that must be performed by the person who hold's the nation's highest office.

OBJECTIVES

After completing this activity, students will be able to:
- list the roles of the U.S. president;
- explain the roles of the U.S. president;
- identify the president's roles in current events;
- evaluate arguments for prioritizing the roles of the president;
- write an effective letter and advice column;
- recognize the responsibilities that come with giving reasoned and thoughtful advice;
- appreciate the responsibilities that come with the office of U.S. president.

LEARNING CONNECTIONS

- Learning Styles: interpersonal, intrapersonal, linguistic

- Skills Mastery: acquiring information, defining/clarifying problems, determining the strength of an argument, drawing conclusions, navigating the Internet, recognizing point of view, solving problems, synthesizing information, writing mastery: describing, writing mastery: persuading
- **Connecting with Past Learning:** Chapter 3, Section 1—discussion of the duties of the executive branch; Chapter 3, Section 3—discussion of executive actions; Chapter 6, Section 3—discussion of the president's role in the legislative process; Chapter 7, Section 1—discussion of the president's roles

PLANNING

Purpose: You may use this activity in combination with teacher-directed lessons for this chapter, as a performance-based assessment of content mastery, or as an enrichment project.

Suggested Time: Plan to spend about six to eight 45-minute class periods on this project. Allow one class period to introduce the activity, discuss the roles of the president of the United States, and organize groups. Give the groups one or two class periods to research the various roles of the president. Set aside one or two periods for student groups to discuss these roles and draft a letter from the president to an advice columnist. Allow one class period for students to read the letters and discuss as a class the possible ways to prioritize these roles. Then allow one class period for students to write an advice column. The final class period will be used for presentation, class discussion, and class voting on the advice column that gives the president the wisest and most practical advice.

Scale of Project: Students will need enough space to meet in groups and to post their letters and advice columns.

Group Size: Organize students into groups of three to six students. Each group will research the various roles of the president, write a letter from the president, and prepare an advice column.

Materials: Students will need paper for the letters and advice columns, and bulletin-board space to post the letters and columns.

Resources: Have students use their textbooks, the Internet, the library, and any other materials that you provide to complete their research. If feasible, students may wish to contact the advice columnist of your local newspaper to gain that person's perspective on advice-column preparation. Similarly, if your school newspaper has an advice columnist, that person may be able to give students some perspective on the task at hand. Encourage students to explore and tap all available sources of information.

Preparation: Before starting the project, make copies of the Planning Guidelines and Project Task Sheet; you will need at least one copy for each group. You may also wish to make copies of the Standards for Evaluation form   which is a project-specific rubric—for students to use in preparing their materials.

IMPLEMENTATION

1. Give students an overview of the activity by describing its five stages. Tell students that they will first list and discuss the roles of the president of the United States. They will then work in groups to research the various roles of the president by analyzing current events. Each group will then write a letter from the president to an advice columnist requesting advice on prioritizing these responsibilities. Then each group will respond to another group's letter in the form of an advice column. Groups will present their columns and then the class as a whole will debate and vote on the most effective and practical column.

2. To begin a discussion of the roles of the U.S. president, have students review Section 1 of Chapter 7, "The Presidential Office." Ask volunteers to list on the chalkboard the roles of the president. *(chief executive, commander in chief, chief legislator, representative of the nation, chief of state, foreign-policy leader, and party leader)* Then ask students to discuss what potential problems and conflicts the president might face in performing these roles. *(For example, the president might face conflicts between political party loyalty and national concerns, and also might face difficulties caused by the need to focus on both foreign and domestic problems.)*

3. Ensure that students understand the following terms: executive, commander in chief, legislator, agenda, representative, state, diplomacy, foreign policy, domestic policy, party. It might be helpful to list the terms on the chalkboard and have students define them. If necessary, have students use the Glossary at the back of the textbook or a dictionary to write the definitions of these terms.

4. Organize the class into groups of three to six students. Distribute copies of the Planning Guidelines and Project Task Sheet to each group and, if you wish, copies of the Standards for Evaluation form. Go over the instructions on the Project Task Sheet to make sure that students understand the assignment. Remind students that the letters should lay out all of the president's responsibilities. They should also express the president's concerns about particular issues and responsibilities, including those to political party, voters, special interests, the public good, and the president's family. Encourage the groups to brainstorm about where to locate the best sources of information about the president's roles.

5. Have student groups begin finding examples from current events that describe the president's roles. Groups might assign members one or two roles each in order to divide up the research. Students should find at least one example of each role. Guide students in speculating how these roles might create challenges for the president in scheduling his or her time, working for the public good, having sufficient information to make important decisions, and balancing family life with work.

6. Once students have completed their research, have each group draft a letter from the president to an advice columnist outlining the president's roles, using examples to describe the range of duties he or she must fulfill. The letter should express the president's concerns about how to prioritize each of these obligations without shortchanging any of them. Students should discuss the challenges of avoiding conflicts of interest and any other time constraints and personal issues that they think might concern the president.

7. Have the groups post their letters on a bulletin board. After students have read the letters, hold a class discussion about the various examples of presidential duties. Encourage students to

express what priority they believe each role should be given.

8. After the discussion is completed, distribute one letter to each group, making sure that no group receives its own letter. Have each group act as an advice columnist and respond to the president's letter. The letters should analyze the importance of each duty, make a list prioritizing the roles, assess how to delegate some of the president's duties, and offer other time-management suggestions for balancing the president's personal responsibilities.

9. After students have completed their columns, post them on the bulletin board for the class to read. Then hold a class discussion regarding the pros and cons of each list of priorities. Have students vote on which advice column they think would best help the president balance these varied responsibilities.

ASSESSMENT

1. Use the Standards for Evaluation form to help you evaluate students' work in creating their letters and advice columns.

2. Individual grades can be based on student participation in research, writing, or class discussion.

3. Alternatively, you can assess student performance by using any or all of the following rubrics from the *Alternative Assessment Handbook* on the *One-Stop Planner CD-ROM:* Rubric 1: Acquiring Information, Rubric 9: Comparing and Contrasting, Rubric 11: Discussions, Rubric 12: Drawing Conclusions, Rubric 14: Group Activity, Rubric 25: Personal Letters, Rubric 30: Research, Rubric 35: Solving Problems, Rubric 40: Writing to Describe, Rubric 43: Writing to Persuade.

PLANNING GUIDELINES

The President's Problem

The president of the United States is being pulled in several different directions at once by the many duties of the presidency. The president desperately needs to prioritize these duties to be able to deal effectively with each task. The president has asked for help from several advisers, but each adviser seems to have a different opinion on which presidential responsibility is of higher priority. To get some impartial advice, the president has faxed a letter to several well-known advice columnists outlining the many responsibilities of the office and requesting an immediate response.

PROJECT TASK SHEET

The President's Letter

Write a letter from the president to an advice columnist that outlines the many roles and responsibilities of the office. Include examples from current events to illustrate exactly what each of the president's roles involves. Be sure to consider the personal responsibilities the president must handle as well, including family obligations, personal health concerns, and religious beliefs.

The Advice Column

Several well-known advice columnists have received an urgent fax from the president of the United States. The president has requested help in prioritizing the various demands on the president's time and attention. Writing as one of the advice columnists, respond to the president's letter. Your advice column should evaluate the importance of each role the president must fulfill, carefully consider any conflicts that might arise between each of these responsibilities, and weigh the president's responsibilities to the nation against those to self and family. Prioritize each role, drafting a daily schedule for the president detailing which matters the president should attend to first. Fully explain in your response your reasons for prioritizing these roles as you do. Be prepared to defend your reasoning against other advice columnists the president may have consulted.

STANDARDS FOR EVALUATION

EXCELLENT

- The group's letter and advice column present a thorough understanding of the roles of the president.
- The group's letter and advice column present a comprehensive analysis of the potential conflicts between the roles of the president.
- All group members participate fully in the research, discussion, writing, and presentation of the letter and advice column.

GOOD

- The group's letter and advice column present a basic understanding of the roles of the president.
- The group's letter and advice column present an analysis of the potential conflicts between the roles of the president.
- All group members participate in the research, discussion, writing, and presentation of the letter and advice column.

ACCEPTABLE

- The group's letter and advice column present an understanding of some of the roles of the president.
- The group's letter and advice column present an analysis of the potential conflicts between some of the roles of the president.
- Most group members participate in the research, discussion, writing, and presentation of the letter and advice column.

UNACCEPTABLE

- The group's letter and advice column fail to show an understanding of the roles of the president.
- The group's letter and advice column do not present any analysis of the potential conflicts between the roles of the president.
- Fewer than half of the group members participate in the research, discussion, writing, and presentation of the letter and advice column.

GOVERNMENT AGENCIES: HOW DO THEY RATE?

GOAL

In this activity students will learn about the independent agencies of the executive branch of government by writing a performance evaluation of an independent agency.

OVERVIEW

This project has four components: group discussion, research, writing a performance evaluation, and class discussion of evaluations. First, the class will list and discuss the functions of the executive branch's independent agencies. Next, each student group will select an independent agency and research its functions and effectiveness. Using their research, the groups each will then write a performance evaluation of the independent agency. Finally, the class will compare the evaluations and make recommendations about how to improve the independent agencies.

OBJECTIVES

After completing this activity, students will be able to:

- identify independent agencies of the executive branch of government;
- describe the main functions of major independent agencies;
- list criteria for evaluating the effectiveness of independent agencies;
- evaluate the effectiveness of selected independent agencies;
- draft a performance evaluation of a particular independent agency;
- rank the functions of an independent agency;
- compare the effectiveness of various independent agencies;
- offer suggestions about how to improve the effectiveness of independent agencies.

LEARNING CONNECTIONS

- Learning Styles: interpersonal, linguistic, logical-mathematical
- Skills Mastery: acquiring information, defining problems, drawing conclusions, judging information, making comparisons, navigating the Internet, presenting data graphically, synthesizing information, writing mastery: describing, writing mastery: persuading
- **Connecting with Past Learning:** Chapter 8, Section 2—discussion of the federal bureaucracy; Chapter 8, Section 3—discussion of the executive branch and the public good

PLANNING

Purpose: You may use this activity in combination with teacher-directed lessons for this chapter, as a performance-based assessment of content mastery, or as an enrichment project.

Suggested Time: Plan to spend about six to eight 45-minute class periods on this project. Allow one class period to introduce the activity, hold a general discussion of independent agencies in the executive branch of government, and organize groups. Give the groups two or three class periods to research an independent agency. Allow two or three days for each group to analyze its information and write a performance evaluation of its independent agency. The final class period should be used for presentation of the groups' performance evaluations and a class discussion.

Scale of Project: Students will need enough room to present their evaluations in front of the class.

Group Size: Organize students into groups of three to four students. Each group will research an independent agency, write a performance-evaluation report about that agency, and present the evaluation to the class.

Materials: Students may need access to a typewriter or computer to prepare the final draft of their performance evaluations. Students might also wish to prepare overhead transparencies or slides to accompany their evaluations.

Resources: Have students use their textbooks, the Internet, the library, and any other materials that you provide to complete their research. If feasible, students may wish to contact professors of government at colleges or universities in your community to learn more about the executive branch's independent agencies. Encourage students to explore and tap all available sources of information.

Preparation: Before starting the project, make copies of the Planning Guidelines and Project Task Sheet; you will need at least one copy for each group. You may also wish to make copies of the Standards for Evaluation form—which is a project-specific rubric—for students to use in preparing their documents.

IMPLEMENTATION

1. Give students an overview of the activity by describing its four stages. Tell students that they will first identify independent agencies of the executive branch of government and discuss their functions. They will then choose one of the independent agencies and work in groups to find out how effective the agency has been in carrying out its assigned functions. Next, each student group will analyze the information it has collected and write a performance evaluation of the independent agency. The student groups will then present their performance evaluations to the class for discussion.

2. To begin a discussion of the independent agencies, have students review Section 2 of Chapter 8, entitled "The Federal Bureaucracy." Ask a volunteer to provide a definition for the term *independent agency.* Then ask individual students to list on the chalkboard the independent agencies mentioned in this section. Also ask them to add to the list any independent agencies that are not mentioned in the textbook but that they are familiar with. Encourage volunteers to discuss what sort of contact, if any, they have had with these agencies. Have students describe the main functions of each of these independent agencies and list the functions on the chalkboard. Guide students in explaining how these agencies help the Executive Office of the President carry out its many responsibilities.

3. Ensure that students understand the following terms: executive branch, bureaucracy, independent agency, regulatory commission, government corporation, public comment, inefficiency, and performance measures. It might be helpful to list the terms on the chalkboard and have students define them. If neces-

sary, have students use the Glossary at the back of the textbook or a dictionary to write the definitions of these terms. Offer clarification of the terms as needed.

4. Organize the class into groups of three to four students. Distribute copies of the Planning Guidelines and Project Task Sheet and, if you wish, copies of the Standards for Evaluation form. Have each group select an independent agency from the list on the chalkboard. You may need to coordinate the selection process so that each group chooses a different independent agency. Then go over the instructions on the Project Task Sheet to make sure that students understand the assignment. Explain that each group will need to find statistical information, news reports, research reports, and other information to determine the main functions of the agency that group members have selected. The groups will then use this information to evaluate how effective their chosen independent agencies are in carrying out their functions.

5. Have students begin researching the independent agencies they have selected. Circulate among the groups to help the members of each group divide up the research fairly. Each student might be responsible for finding a specific type of information or for researching a specific function. Encourage students to contact the public information branch of the agency directly or to review its World Wide Web site for a description of its functions. Guide them in locating statistics that reflect how well the agency is carrying out its assigned functions. They might also contact or review reports from "watchdog" groups that have evaluated the agency.

6. Once students have completed their research, have student groups discuss and analyze the information they have collected. Remind them that grades are a type of performance measure. They are, in effect, grading the independent agency, just as their work is graded by teachers. Ask the groups to rate the effectiveness of each of the agency's functions using the rating system shown on the Project Task Sheet. Then have the members of each group work together to write a performance evaluation of the independent agency. Explain that the performance evaluation should describe the main functions of the agency, provide an overall rating of the

agency, present evidence that explains how well the agency carries out its functions, and suggest ways that the agency can improve its efficiency and effectiveness in carrying out its designated functions.

7. Next, have the groups present their performance evaluations to the class. Either have a volunteer from each group present the entire report or have each student present one function of the chosen agency. After all of the groups have presented their performance evaluations, have the class rank the agencies in order of efficiency.

8. Finally, use the performance evaluations and the agency rankings as the basis of a class discussion on the federal bureaucracy. Have students evaluate which of the suggested recommendations seems most feasible and practical for improving the efficiency and effectiveness of the federal bureaucracy. Consider having students work individually or cooperatively to write letters to the independent agencies or to the White House outlining their recommendations for change.

ASSESSMENT

1. Use the Standards for Evaluation form to help you evaluate students' performance evaluations.

2. Individual grades can be based on student participation in research, writing, presentation, or class discussion.

3. An option for additional individual assessment is to grade students' letters to the independent agencies or to the White House.

4. Alternatively, you can assess student performance by using any or all of the following rubrics from the *Alternative Assessment Handbook* on the *One-Stop Planner CD-ROM:* Rubric 1: Acquiring Information, Rubric 5: Business Letters, Rubric 7: Charts, Rubric 9: Comparing and Contrasting, Rubric 11: Discussions, Rubric 12: Drawing Conclusions, Rubric 14: Group Activity, Rubric 16: Judging Information, Rubric 29: Presentations, Rubric 30: Research, Rubric 35: Solving Problems, Rubric 40: Writing to Describe.

PLANNING GUIDELINES

Several recent newspaper articles have reported that the executive branch's independent agencies are operating inefficiently. One well-known senator claims that the agencies waste tax dollars and should be dissolved. Your assignment is to investigate the senator's claims. Choose an independent agency, and research its main functions and how effective it has been in carrying out these functions. Begin by evaluating the agency's performance based on information from watchdog groups, media or research reports, statistics and other information provided by the agency, and your own observations. Then write a performance evaluation that assesses how well the agency is working. The evaluation should include recommendations that answer the senator's concerns.

PROJECT TASK SHEET

Drafting a Performance Evaluation

Begin the performance evaluation with a brief description of the independent agency and its functions. Use the rating scale below to evaluate each of the agency's functions. Be sure to provide statistical or other evidence for your rating. You might prepare a chart like the one below to lay out your findings. Determine an overall rating for your independent agency by averaging the ratings of each function. To conclude your report, answer the question "Do you think the agency operates effectively?" Then make any recommendations that you think are necessary to improve the agency.

Your report should be about 250 to 500 words. When preparing the evaluation, remember that your group will present your performance evaluation to the rest of the class. Prepare graphs or charts that can be displayed or handed out during the presentation. After all of the performance evaluations have been presented to the class, rank each of the agencies in order of effectiveness.

Rating Scale:
- **4** = Excellent
- **3** = Strong
- **2** = Adequate
- **1** = Weak
- **0** = Unable to Judge

Example:
Federal Dirt and Soil Agency

Function	Rating	Evidence
Conserve soil on public lands	1	More than 50 percent of soil has eroded from public land; there are only two Dirt Agents per state to carry out this function
Keep soil on public lands free of pollutants	2	Most public lands are free of pollutants; however, Soil Rangers argue that there is not enough money in their budget to clean up the worst sites

STANDARDS FOR EVALUATION

EXCELLENT

- The group's performance evaluation presents a thorough description of the independent agency's functions.
- The group's performance evaluation presents a thorough analysis of how well the independent agency carries out its assigned functions.
- All group members participate fully in the research, discussion, analysis, writing, and presentation of the performance evaluation.

GOOD

- The group's performance evaluation presents an adequate understanding of the independent agency's functions.
- The group's performance evaluation presents a basic understanding of how well the independent agency carries out its assigned functions.
- All group members participate in the research, discussion, analysis, writing, and presentation of the performance evaluation.

ACCEPTABLE

- The group's performance evaluation lists most of the independent agency's functions.
- The group's performance evaluation analyzes how well the independent agency carries out most of its assigned functions.
- Most group members participate in the research, discussion, analysis, writing, and presentation of the performance evaluation.

UNACCEPTABLE

- The group's performance evaluation fails to describe the independent agency's functions.
- The group's performance evaluation fails to analyze how well the independent agency performs its assigned functions.
- Fewer than half of the group members participate in the research, discussion, analysis, writing, and presentation of the performance evaluation.

YOUR TAX SYSTEM AT WORK

GOAL

In this activity students will learn about how federal tax laws affect family finances by researching recent changes in tax laws, determining a fictional family's federal income tax, and preparing a family budget.

OVERVIEW

This project has five components: discussion, research, determining a fictional family's income tax, preparing a family budget, and final discussion and evaluation. First, students will participate in a discussion about how the government generates revenue through the federal tax system. Next, student groups will research recent changes in U.S. tax laws. The groups each will then use Internal Revenue Service (IRS) tax forms to determine a fictional family's income tax. Next, the groups will use their collected information to prepare a family budget. Finally, students will discuss the impact of federal tax laws on individuals and families.

OBJECTIVES

After completing this activity, students will be able to:
- identify the ways that the federal government generates income;
- list the major types of federal taxes;
- discuss federal tax laws;
- identify the most recent changes in federal tax laws;
- describe federal income tax forms;
- prepare a family budget;
- analyze how federal tax laws affect a family budget;
- explain the relationship between economic policy and the public good.

LEARNING CONNECTIONS

- Learning Styles: interpersonal, linguistic, logical-mathematical

- Skills Mastery: acquiring information, defining problems, determining cause and effect, drawing conclusions, judging information, making comparisons, navigating the Internet, presenting data graphically, solving problems, synthesizing information, understanding cause and effect

- *Connecting with Past Learning:* Chapter 9, Section 1—discussion of revenue raising; Chapter 9, Section 3—discussion of the federal budget

PLANNING

Purpose: You may use this activity in combination with teacher-directed lessons for this chapter, as a performance-based assessment of content mastery, or as an enrichment project.

Suggested Time: Plan to spend about six to eight 45-minute class periods on this project. Allow one class period to introduce the activity, organize the students into groups, and hold a class discussion on the federal tax system. Give the groups two class periods to research the most recent changes in federal tax laws. Set aside one or two class periods for the student groups to determine their assigned family's federal income tax. Then give student groups one or two class periods to create a family budget and present their work on posters. The final class period should be used for students to display their work, review other groups' posters, and discuss how federal taxes affect family budgets.

Scale of Project: Students will need enough room to meet in groups of four to six and enough wall or hallway space to hang and display their posters.

Group Size: Organize the class into four groups of four to six students. Each group will represent a fictional family.

Materials: Students will need poster board and other art supplies to illustrate their fictional family's tax and budget information.

Resources: Have students use their textbooks, the Internet, the library, and any other materials that you provide to complete their research. If feasible, students may wish to contact representatives of the Internal Revenue Service, accountants, financial planners, or financial counselors working in your community. Encourage students to explore and tap all available sources of information.

Preparation: Before starting the project, make copies of the Planning Guidelines and Project Task Sheet; you will need at least one copy for each group. You should also make at least four copies of the most recent Internal Revenue Service Form 1040A or Form 1040EZ, which can be downloaded from the IRS World Wide Web site (http://www.irs.ustreas.gov) or found at your local library. You may also wish to make copies of the Standards for Evaluation form— which is a project-specific rubric—for students to use in preparing their presentations.

IMPLEMENTATION

1. Give students an overview of the activity by describing its five stages. Tell students that they will begin the activity by discussing the federal tax system. They will then work in groups to research recent changes in U.S. tax laws. Students will then use tax forms from the Internal Revenue Service to determine a fictional family's federal income tax. Groups will use this information to prepare a family budget. Each group will then present its research, tax form, and budget to the class. The activity will conclude with a general discussion of the effects of the tax system on the four families.

2. To begin the discussion of the federal tax system, have students review Section 1 of Chapter 9, entitled "Raising Revenue." Ask students to provide examples of how the federal government generates revenue from taxes, and list students' examples on the chalkboard. *(Examples may include corporate income tax, individual income tax, excise tax, estate tax, gift tax, and customs duties.)* Ask volunteers to provide real-life examples of how they are affected by federal income taxes.

3. Ensure that students understand the following terms: revenue, tax, exemption, deduction, corporate income tax, social insurance tax, excise tax, estate tax, gift tax, customs duty, progressive tax, regressive tax, standard of living, and

budget. It might be helpful to list these terms on the chalkboard and have volunteers supply definitions of each term. If necessary, have students use the Glossary at the back of the textbook or a dictionary to write the definitions of these terms.

4. Organize the class into four groups of four to six students. Distribute copies of the Planning Guidelines, the Project Task Sheet, the Internal Revenue forms, and, if you wish, copies of the Standards for Evaluation form. Go over the instructions on the Planning Guidelines to make sure that students understand the assignment. Assign or have each student group select one of the family profiles listed on the Project Task Sheet. Tell students that the family profiles provide only a rough sketch of each family's expenses. The groups will need to add details to their family profiles to make them more realistic and descriptive. Group members may want to describe additional family expenses, investments, and savings.

5. Have student groups begin researching recent changes in federal tax laws that affect their fictional families. Guide students in focusing on changes in credits for dependent children and educational expenses, reductions in the capital gains tax on the sale of homes, and changes to gift taxes. Suggest that students look at personal finance magazines, the Internal Revenue Service World Wide Web site, and newspapers to learn about recent changes in tax laws.

6. Once students have completed their research, have each group review the income profile for its assigned family. Tell group members to add additional, realistic details to the income profile that will affect the federal income tax the family owes. Then have students use the IRS forms to determine the family's federal income tax. Keep in mind that the goal of the activity is to generate discussion rather than to reach a "correct" answer. Groups may assume that no taxes have been withheld from their income.

7. Student groups should then use this information to create a yearly budget for their families. Remind students that they can add additional savings and expenses as long as their families do not go into debt. They might include school, entertainment, vacation, insurance, emergency funds, and other expenses. The groups should each create a pie chart that shows the percentages of the total income budgeted to pay their

various expenses, including federal income taxes.

8. Next, have each group display its financial information on a poster. The posters should describe the group's family, recent changes in tax laws that affect the family, the family's tax form, and a detailed look at the family's budget. Display the posters in class and have each group present its findings.

9. Conclude the activity by leading the class in a discussion of the effects of federal income taxes on a family's budget. Encourage students to respond to the following questions: How much money did these families have left over after they paid taxes and expenses? How far does their after-tax income stretch? How do you think the recent changes in tax laws affect your own family? Would you recommend changes in the tax laws after seeing how taxes affect the fictional families? If so, what changes would you recommend? If you recommend that the government reduce taxes, how will government raise sufficient revenue to pay for programs and services?

ASSESSMENT

1. Use the Standards for Evaluation form to help you evaluate students' work in researching recent changes in tax laws, figuring out a fictional family's income tax, and creating a family budget.

2. Individual grades can be based on student participation in research, tax calculation, budgeting, or class discussion.

3. Alternatively, you can assess student performance by using any or all of the following rubrics from the *Alternative Assessment Handbook* on the *One Stop Planner CD–ROM:* Rubric 1: Acquiring Information, Rubric 6: Cause and Effect, Rubric 7: Charts, Rubric 11: Discussions, Rubric 12: Drawing Conclusions, Rubric 14: Group Activity, Rubric 28: Posters, Rubric 29: Presentations, Rubric 30: Research, Rubric 35: Solving Problems.

PLANNING GUIDELINES

April 15: Tax Time!

April 15—the deadline for filing federal income taxes—is fast approaching, and the Abada, Binet, Carter, and Dolbert families need to determine how much federal income tax they owe. They do not know if the federal government has made any recent changes to the tax system, so they will need to do a bit of research. As a member of one of these families, use local tax hotlines, personal finance magazines, newspapers, and the Internal Revenue Service (IRS) World Wide Web site to find out if there are any recent changes in the U.S. tax laws that will affect your family.

Then, using the Internal Revenue Service's 1040 form and the family profiles below, determine how much money your family owes the federal government. Next, use the family profile information and tax owed to create a detailed yearly budget for your family. Create a poster that contains your tax form, the detailed budget, and a summary of the recent changes in tax laws that affect your family. Illustrate the poster with pie charts, graphs, or other graphics to show how federal income taxes affect your family's finances.

PROJECT TASK SHEET

Family Budget: The Abadas

The Abada family income is $60,000 per year. The Abadas have four children and spend about $1,000 a month on food. They pay $1,000 a month for the mortgage on their home. They buy about $10,000 in goods each year. They took one trip abroad and brought back $2,000 worth of souvenirs.

Family Budget: The Binets

The Binet family income is $40,000 per year. They have no children and spend about $700 a month on food. The Binets buy $4,000 per year in goods and spend $1,000 a month for their house payment. They won $10,000 in the lottery this year.

Family Budget: The Carters

The Carter family income is $18,000 per year. They have two children and spend about $400 a month on food. They buy $2,000 per year in goods and pay $500 per month on rent for their two-bedroom apartment. Ms. Carter recently purchased a new puppy for the children. The Carters inherited $10,000 this year.

Family Budget: The Dolberts

The Dolbert family income is $30,000 per year. They have just sold their large house for a profit of $50,000. They are renting a small apartment for $600 a month. Their children are grown and no longer live with them. They spend $400 a month on food. They buy about $5,000 in goods per year and spend about $2,000 on travel. One of their children has just asked for a loan of $10,000.

STANDARDS FOR EVALUATION

EXCELLENT

- The group's research presents a thorough understanding of how recent changes in tax laws affect their assigned family.
- The group's tax form and budget are complete and show a full understanding of how tax laws affect their assigned family.
- All group members participate fully in the research, calculation of taxes, creation of the family budget, and discussion of how federal income taxes affect individuals.

GOOD

- The group's research presents a complete understanding of how recent changes in tax laws affect their assigned family.
- The group's tax form and budget show a good understanding of how tax laws affect their assigned family.
- All group members participate in the research, calculation of taxes, creation of the family budget, and discussion of how federal income taxes affect individuals.

ACCEPTABLE

- The group's research presents a basic understanding of how recent changes in tax laws affect their assigned family.
- The group's tax form and budget show how tax laws affect their assigned family.
- Most group members participate in the research, calculation of taxes, creation of the family budget, and discussion of how federal income taxes affect individuals.

UNACCEPTABLE

- The group's research fails to present a basic understanding of how recent changes in tax laws affect their assigned family.
- The group's tax form and budget do not reflect an understanding of how tax laws affect their assigned family.
- Fewer than half of the group members participate in the research, calculation of taxes, creation of the family budget, and discussion of how federal income taxes affect individuals.

GLOBAL GIVING: ASKING FOR AID

GOAL

In this activity students will learn about U.S. aid to foreign countries by drafting a mock aid proposal from a foreign country to the United States.

OVERVIEW

This project has five components: discussion, research, proposal writing, presentation of proposals, and discussion and voting to determine which country most needs aid assistance from the United States. First, students will participate in a discussion about U.S. aid to foreign countries. Next, student groups each will research a foreign country to determine why that country might need U.S. aid. Using the research findings, each group will prepare a mock proposal requesting aid from the United States. The groups will then present their proposals orally to the class. Finally, the class will evaluate the proposals and vote to decide which country most needs U.S. aid.

OBJECTIVES

After completing this activity, students will be able to:
- identify types of U.S. foreign aid;
- identify the methods by which the U.S. government gives aid to foreign countries;
- list the reasons for which the United States gives aid to foreign countries;
- conduct cross-cultural research;
- draft a foreign-aid proposal;
- prepare arguments in favor of a proposal;
- present an effective oral argument;
- evaluate a variety of foreign-aid proposals;
- weigh the needs of various countries;
- assess how best to allot U.S. foreign aid.

LEARNING CONNECTIONS

- Learning Styles: interpersonal, linguistic, logical-mathematical
- Skills Mastery: acquiring information, defining/clarifying problems, determining the strength of an argument, drawing conclusions, judging information, making comparisons, navigating the Internet, presenting data graphically, recognizing point of view, writing mastery: informing, writing mastery: persuading
- *Connecting with Past Learning:* Chapter 7, Section 1: discussion of the president's role as foreign-policy leader; Chapter 7, Section 2— power of the president to make executive agreements involving economic assistance to foreign countries; Chapter 10, Section 1: discussion of U.S. foreign-policy goals; Chapter 10, Section 4—discussion of foreign aid and foreign alliances

PLANNING

Purpose: You may use this activity in combination with teacher-directed lessons for this chapter, as a performance-based assessment of content mastery, or as an enrichment project.

Suggested Time: Plan to spend about five to eight 45-minute class periods on this project. Allow one class period to introduce the activity, hold a general class discussion on foreign aid, and organize students into groups. Give the groups two or three class periods to research their assigned foreign country. Allow one or two class periods for the groups to draft their foreign-aid proposals. Set aside one or two more class periods for students to present their proposals and for the class to determine which country most needs aid from the United States.

Scale of Project: Students will need enough room to meet in groups and to present their foreign-aid proposals in front of the class.

Group Size: Organize the class into five groups. The number of students in each group will depend on the overall class size. Each group will research and write a foreign-aid proposal for one of the following countries: Afghanistan, Cambodia, Haiti, Lebanon, or Sudan.

Materials: Students will need materials to draft and present their proposals. Groups may simply create copies of their proposal to hand out during their presentations, or they may provide posters, charts, or other audiovisual materials to help explain why their assigned country would benefit from U.S. foreign aid.

Resources: Have students use their textbooks, the Internet, the library, and any other materials that you provide to complete their research. If feasible, students may wish to contact professors of government, geography, and/or sociology at colleges or universities in your community to learn more about their assigned countries. Encourage students to explore and tap all available sources of information.

Preparation: Before starting the project, make copies of the Planning Guidelines and Project Task Sheet; you will need at least one copy for each group. You may also wish to make copies of the Standards for Evaluation form—which is a project-specific rubric—for students to use in preparing their presentations.

IMPLEMENTATION

1. Give students an overview of the activity by describing its five stages. Tell students that they will first discuss U.S. aid to foreign countries. They will then work in groups to research a particular country. After the members of each group have determined the country's most pressing needs, they will write a proposal requesting aid from the United States. Each group will then prepare and present to the class an oral version of its proposal. After all of the aid proposals have been presented, the class will discuss the needs of each country and vote to determine which country should receive aid from the United States.

2. To begin a discussion of U.S. foreign aid, have students review Section 4 of Chapter 10, entitled "Foreign Aid and Alliances." Ask students to identify the reasons why the U.S. government has given out aid to foreign countries. Write students' responses on the chalkboard. *(Reasons may include the following: promote democracy, encourage economic growth, concern for public health issues, humanitarian reasons, concern for the global environment.)* Then ask students to identify the forms that U.S. foreign aid has taken. *(Responses may include monetary, military, technological, and technical advisers.)*

3. Ensure that students understand the following terms: foreign aid, humanitarianism, democracy, and U.S. Agency for International Devel-

opment. It might be helpful to list the terms on the chalkboard and have students define them. If necessary, have students use the Glossary at the back of the textbook or a dictionary to write the definitions of these terms. Offer clarification of the terms as needed.

4. Organize the class into five groups and assign each group one of the following countries: Afghanistan, Cambodia, Haiti, Lebanon, or Sudan. Distribute copies of the Planning Guidelines and the Project Task Sheet and, if you wish, copies of the Standards for Evaluation form. Go over the instructions on the Project Task Sheet to make sure that students understand the components of the assignment. Explain that the overall objective of this activity is to identify problems in other countries that the United States works to solve by giving foreign-aid assistance. Make sure that students identify all of the information they will need to find in their research.

5. Have the groups begin researching their respective countries. Encourage students to locate and use a wide range of available resources to determine what needs their assigned country may have. Tell the groups that they should make use of at least three different sources when researching their countries. If students have access to the Internet, guide them in finding the World Wide Web site for the U.S. Agency for International Development (http://www.usaid.gov), which has a wealth of information on this topic. You might also suggest that students contact representatives from foreign consulates for more information on their assigned countries.

6. Once students have completed their research, have each group write a formal proposal requesting aid from the United States. Tell the groups to limit their proposal to two pages. Their proposals should begin with a brief overview of the country. The proposals should then list major problems in each of the following areas: Government, Economy, Environment, Public Health, Military, and the Judicial System. For each of these areas, the proposal should explain the type of aid requested and how this aid will help solve the problems. The proposal should conclude by giving reasons why granting such aid would meet U.S. foreign-policy goals. Encourage students to rehearse an oral version of the arguments contained in their proposals.

7. Next, have the groups present their formal proposals to the class. Have each student in the group argue the need for U.S. aid in one particular area, either government, economy, environment, or some other area. Ask the groups to limit their presentations to no more than 10 minutes each so that all groups can present their proposals in one class period.

8. After all proposals have been presented, have the class hold a mock meeting of the U.S. Agency for International Development. Tell students that the United States has sufficient resources to help only *one* country this year. Then lead the class in a general discussion to evaluate each of the aid proposals. Guide students in weighing the most pressing needs of each country and the goals of U.S. foreign policy. They should answer the following question: Which country's aid request is most consistent with U.S. foreign-policy goals? End the activity with a vote to decide which country will receive U.S. foreign aid this year.

ASSESSMENT

1. Use the Standards for Evaluation form to help you evaluate students' work in writing and presenting a foreign-aid proposal.

2. Individual grades can be based on student participation in research, writing, presentation, or class discussion.

3. Alternatively, you can assess student performance by using any or all of the following rubrics from the *Alternative Assessment Handbook* on the *One-Stop Planner CD-ROM:* Rubric 1: Acquiring Information, Rubric 7: Charts, Rubric 9: Comparing and Contrasting, Rubric 11: Discussions, Rubric 12: Drawing Conclusions, Rubric 14: Group Activity, Rubric 16: Judging Information, Rubric 24: Oral Presentations, Rubric 28: Posters, Rubric 30: Research, Rubric 35: Solving Problems, Rubric 43: Writing to Persuade.

PLANNING GUIDELINES

Your country has just been informed that, due to budget cuts, the United States will grant foreign aid to only *one* country this year. Five countries desperately need this aid. As a representative of one of these countries, your group has been asked to research the most urgent needs of your country. Your country may need U.S. aid in the following areas: Government, Economy, Environment, Public Health, Military, and the Judicial System. After you determine what problems your country has in each of these areas, prepare a formal proposal requesting aid from the United States. Your group will then present this proposal to the class. Finally, the class will hold a mock meeting of the U.S. Agency for International Development to decide which of the five countries most needs U.S. aid.

PROJECT TASK SHEET

Aid Proposal

You will research and draft an aid proposal for one of the countries below:

- Afghanistan
- Cambodia
- Haiti
- Lebanon
- Sudan

Research: Use the library, the Internet, international aid organizations, foreign consulates, and other resources to gain an understanding of the needs of your assigned country in the following areas: Government, Economy, Environment, Public Health, Military, and the Judicial System. Use at least three sources to gather information about your country. Be sure to find out how U.S. aid will help solve your country's problems in each of these areas and what specific goals your country hopes to achieve with U.S. aid.

Aid Proposal: Once you have completed your research, write a proposal requesting aid from the United States. First, present a brief overview of your assigned country—its government, economy, geography, religion, and society. Then describe the areas in which your country needs foreign aid. Explain the type of aid that would help solve these problems, such as economic aid, military aid, technology, or expert advisers. Conclude by arguing why granting such aid will fulfill U.S. foreign-policy goals. Limit your proposal to two pages, and be sure to list the sources you consulted. Remember that only one country will receive aid from the United States this year, so make your proposal count!

Presentation: When your proposal is complete, your group will present it to the class. Have each student present the needs for a particular area. Each student should present one of the group's arguments for how a particular problem can be solved with U.S. aid.

Discussion: After all of the proposals have been presented, the class will hold a mock meeting of the U.S. Agency for International Development (USAID) to discuss which country most needs U.S. aid. Rather than represent your assigned country, you will now play the role of a USAID staffer to objectively weigh the needs of each country. Consider which country has the most pressing needs. You will also need to evaluate the aid proposals in light of the goals of U.S. foreign policy. After you have discussed each proposal, vote to determine which country should receive U.S. aid this year.

STANDARDS FOR EVALUATION

EXCELLENT

- The group's proposal demonstrates a thorough understanding of the needs of the assigned country and how these needs can be addressed.
- The group's proposal demonstrates a thorough understanding of the objectives and workings of U.S. foreign-aid policy.
- All group members participate fully in the research, writing, and presentation of the foreign-aid proposal.

GOOD

- The group's proposal demonstrates a complete understanding of the needs of the assigned country and how these needs can be addressed.
- The group's proposal demonstrates a good understanding of the objectives and workings of U.S. foreign-aid policy.
- All group members participate in the research, writing, and presentation of the foreign-aid proposal.

ACCEPTABLE

- The group's proposal demonstrates some understanding of the needs of the assigned country and how these needs can be addressed.
- The group's proposal demonstrates some understanding of the objectives and workings of U.S. foreign-aid policy.
- Most group members participate in the research, writing, and presentation of the foreign-aid proposal.

UNACCEPTABLE

- The group's proposal fails to demonstrate an understanding of the needs of the assigned country and how these needs can be addressed.
- The group's proposal fails to demonstrate an understanding of the objectives and workings of U.S. foreign-aid policy.
- Fewer than half of the group members participate in the research, writing, and presentation of the foreign-aid proposal.

THE SUPREME COURT BRIEFING BOOK

GOAL

In this activity students will learn about the justices of the U.S. Supreme Court by creating a Supreme Court briefing book, or yearbook, that includes photographs and brief biographies of the justices of the current Supreme Court.

OVERVIEW

This project has five components: group discussion, research, biography writing, creation of the briefing book, and presentation and discussion of the briefing book. First, students will participate in a class discussion about the structure and function of the Supreme Court. Then the student groups will locate photographs of their assigned justices and research their career and biographical details and past Supreme Court decisions. Next, the groups each will use their research findings to write a biography of their assigned justice. The class will then combine the biographies into a Supreme Court briefing book. Finally, each group will present its section of the briefing book to the class, and the class will use the information contained in the briefing book to analyze the current political balance of the Supreme Court.

OBJECTIVES

After completing this activity, students will be able to:
- identify the current justices of the Supreme Court;
- research past decisions of the Supreme Court;
- analyze past decisions of the Supreme Court;
- discuss biographical and career details of each Supreme Court justice;
- identify the legal views of the Supreme Court justices;
- evaluate whether the justices' Supreme Court decisions express a certain political viewpoint;
- characterize the current political balance of the Supreme Court;
- analyze the role that politics plays in the Supreme Court;

- write a biography;
- create a briefing book, or yearbook.

LEARNING CONNECTIONS

- Learning Styles: interpersonal, linguistic, logical-mathematical
- Skills Mastery: acquiring information, drawing conclusions, judging information, making comparisons, navigating the Internet, recognizing point of view, synthesizing information, writing mastery: describing
- ***Connecting with Past Learning:*** Chapter 3, Section 1—discussion of the judicial branch of government and judicial review; Chapter 3, Section 3—discussion of the relationship between Supreme Court decisions and the flexibility of the U.S. Constitution; Chapter 11, Section 1—discussion of the lower courts; Chapter 11, Section 2—discussion of the Supreme Court; Chapter 11, Section 3—discussion of the courts and the public good

PLANNING

Purpose: You may use this activity in combination with teacher-directed lessons for this chapter, as a performance-based assessment of content mastery, or as an enrichment project.

Suggested Time: Plan to spend about six to eight 45-minute class periods on this project. Allow one class period to introduce the activity, hold a class discussion of the Supreme Court, and organize the students into groups. Give the groups two to three class periods to research their assigned Supreme Court justice. Allow one or two class periods for the groups to write a biography of their assigned justice. Also allow the groups one class period to combine their biographies into a Supreme Court briefing book. You may need additional preparation time to bind the briefing book and distribute copies to the class. Use the final class period for students to present their biographies and discuss the current political balance of the Supreme Court.

Scale of Project: Students will need enough room to meet in groups. Because of the large number of groups needed for this activity, you may wish to schedule time in a larger area than that provided by your classroom, such as the cafeteria or a large meeting room. This may help keep the groups from being distracted by the noise generated by nine groups in discussion.

Group Size: Organize the class into nine groups. Group size will depend on overall class size. Each group will research one of the current Supreme Court justices.

Materials: Students will need materials such as paper, and access to a word processor and a photocopy machine to assemble and distribute the Supreme Court briefing book. They may also need binding materials, depending on how elaborate you wish the briefing book to be.

Resources: Have students use their textbooks, the Internet, the library, and any other materials that you provide to complete their research. If students have access to the Internet, they can read about Supreme Court justices and their cases at Cornell University's Legal Information Institute's World Wide Web site (http://supct.law.cornell.edu/supct/). Encourage students to explore and tap all available sources of information.

Preparation: Before starting the project, make copies of the Planning Guidelines and Project Task Sheet; you will need at least one copy for each group. You may also wish to make copies of the Standards for Evaluation form—which is a project-specific rubric—for students to use in preparing their materials.

IMPLEMENTATION

1. Give students an overview of the activity by describing its five stages. Tell students that they will first discuss the justices who make up the Supreme Court and their roles. They will then work with their groups to locate photographs of the current Court justices and research their biographical details and past Supreme Court decisions. The groups will use this information to write short biographies of their assigned justices. When the biographies are completed, the groups will assemble them into a Supreme Court briefing book. Finally, student groups will present their biographies and discuss the legal philosophy and political balance of the current Supreme Court.

2. To begin a discussion of the Supreme Court, have students review Section 2 of Chapter 11, entitled "The Supreme Court." Have students explain the purpose of the Supreme Court, including what cases the justices hear and what their position is in the U.S. judicial system. Then ask students to describe the structure of the Supreme Court, including how many justices there are and how they reach a decision about a case presented before them. Then ask students to identify the current Supreme Court justices, and list students' responses on the chalkboard. Have a volunteer identify which of the nine justices listed on the chalkboard is the current chief justice of the Supreme Court.

3. Ensure that students understand the following terms: chief justice of the Supreme Court, law clerk, strict constructionist, loose constructionist, majority opinion, concurring opinion, dissenting opinion, judicial restraint, judicial activism, conservative, and liberal. It might be helpful to list the terms on the chalkboard and have the students define them. If necessary, have students use the Glossary at the back of the textbook or a dictionary to write the definitions of these terms.

4. Organize the class into nine groups and assign each group one of the current Supreme Court justices. Distribute copies of the Planning Guidelines and the Project Task Sheet and, if you wish, copies of the Standards for Evaluation form. Go over the instructions on the Project Task Sheet to make sure that students understand the assignment. Emphasize that students will need to determine each Supreme Court justice's legal philosophy to include in the biographies.

5. Have the groups begin researching their assigned justices. Students should determine if there are any issues that are of particular interest to their justices. Circulate among the groups as they conduct their research to make sure that they are answering the following questions: Is the justice conservative or liberal in his or her legal philosophy? Is the justice a strict constructionist or a loose constructionist? Does the justice tend usually to vote with a certain group of justices? Also make sure that students locate a photograph of each Supreme Court justice that can be copied and included in the briefing book.

6. Once students have completed their research, have the members of each group write a short biographical sketch of their assigned justice. Tell students to limit each biographical sketch to between two and four pages. They should include such biographical details as the justice's age, when he or she was appointed, by whom he or she was appointed, the justice's legal thinking and political views, and any special areas of interest the justice may have. In addition, each biography should summarize an important decision written by the assigned justice that outlines his or her political philosophy. Students should also include a photograph of the justice and any additional information they think would provide a clearer picture of the justice.

7. After all biographies are complete, have students assemble them into a Supreme Court briefing book. If possible, make a copy of the briefing book for each student.

8. After the briefing book is assembled and distributed, groups should present the highlights of their justice's biography to the class. End the activity with a discussion of the political makeup of the current Supreme Court. Have students discuss whether the Court is conservative or liberal. You might ask the following

questions to spark further discussion: If students were to appoint another justice to balance the political scales of the Court, would they appoint a liberal justice or a conservative justice? Do politics have a place in the courtroom? You may wish to post a copy of the briefing book in the classroom for future reference. Perhaps your school library may wish to include a copy of the briefing book on its reference shelf.

ASSESSMENT

1. Use the Standards for Evaluation form to help you evaluate students' work in writing biographies for the Supreme Court briefing book.

2. Individual grades can be based on student participation in research, writing, presentation, or class discussion.

3. Alternatively, you can assess student performance by using any or all of the following rubrics from the *Alternative Assessment Handbook* on the *One-Stop Planner CD-ROM:* Rubric 1: Acquiring Information, Rubric 4: Biographies, Rubric 11: Discussions, Rubric 12: Drawing Conclusions, Rubric 14: Group Activity, Rubric 29: Presentations, Rubric 30: Research, Rubric 40: Writing to Describe.

PLANNING GUIDELINES

You are a law clerk for the law firm of Jay, Marshall, and Warren. The attorneys in your firm will soon argue a case before the U.S. Supreme Court. Your firm has asked you and several other clerks to research the current members of the Supreme Court. Your objective is to provide a clear picture of the personal background, career highlights, and legal thinking of each justice. You and the other law clerks must find a photograph and write a short biography of each justice. You will then assemble the photographs and biographies in a briefing book, or yearbook. With this briefing book, the lawyers in your firm who will be arguing before the Supreme Court will be able to recognize each justice, understand the past decisions of each justice, and identify the political balance of the current Supreme Court.

PROJECT TASK SHEET

Research: Each of the law clerk teams will be responsible for researching one justice. Use your textbook, the Internet, the library, and other available resources to find a photograph of your assigned justice. In addition, you should find out what year your justice was appointed, by which president the justice was appointed, and what are his or her career highlights. You should also research your justice's legal philosophy to help answer the following questions: Does your justice have any particular issues that interest him or her? Can you label your justice as a conservative or a liberal? As a strict constructionist or a loose constructionist? Does your justice tend to vote with particular justices? It will be useful to locate and summarize one of the majority opinions written by your justice that explains his or her legal thinking.

Writing: Once you have completed your research, write a biography of your justice. Limit your biography to between two and four pages. The biography should include the research detailed above, including a photograph of the justice.

Briefing Book: When the biographies are complete, assemble them to form a Supreme Court briefing book, or yearbook. Each group will present its biography to the class by summarizing the justice's career highlights and legal thinking.

Discussion: The class should then synthesize the information presented to decide what the political makeup of the current Supreme Court is. Try to answer the following questions: Is the current Court conservative or liberal? If you were to appoint another justice to balance the political scales of the Court, would you appoint a liberal or conservative justice? A loose constructionist or a strict constructionist? Do you think that justices should demonstrate any political views at all?

STANDARDS FOR EVALUATION

EXCELLENT

- The group's biography shows a thorough understanding of the career highlights of the assigned justice.
- The group's biography shows a complete understanding of the legal and political views of the justice.
- All group members participate fully in the research, writing, and presentation of the biography.

GOOD

- The group's biography shows a good understanding of the career highlights of the assigned justice.
- The group's biography shows a good understanding of the legal and political views of the justice.
- All group members participate in the research, writing, and presentation of the biography.

ACCEPTABLE

- The group's biography shows some understanding of the career highlights of the assigned justice.
- The group's biography shows some understanding of the legal and political views of the justice.
- Most group members participate in the research, writing, and presentation of the biography.

UNACCEPTABLE

- The group's biography fails to show an understanding of the career highlights of the assigned justice.
- The group's biography fails to show an understanding of the legal and political views of the justice.
- Some group members participate in the research, writing, and presentation of the biography.

YOUR DAY IN TEEN COURT

GOAL

In this activity students will learn about the U.S. legal system by participating in a mock teen court trial.

OVERVIEW

This project has four components: group discussion, research, mock teen court trial, and final class discussion and evaluations. First, students will discuss the U.S. legal system as it relates to teenagers, including juvenile crimes and teen courts. They will then work in groups to research teen courts and write guidelines for their assigned teen court roles. When their research is complete, students will participate in a mock teen court trial. Finally, students will hold a discussion about the outcome of the teen court trial and the effectiveness of teen courts.

OBJECTIVES

After completing this activity, students will be able to:
- describe how the U.S. legal system treats juvenile crimes;
- explain the purpose of teen courts;
- discuss how teen courts work;
- identify and describe the roles of the main people involved in a trial;
- present evidence and legal arguments;
- evaluate evidence and legal arguments;
- describe how juries reach their verdicts;
- decide appropriate punishments for juvenile crimes;
- evaluate the effectiveness of teen courts.

LEARNING CONNECTIONS

- Learning Styles: interpersonal, linguistic
- Skills Mastery: acquiring information, determining the strength of an argument, distinguishing fact and opinion, drawing conclusions, judging information, navigating the Internet, recognizing point of view, solving problems, understanding cause and effect

- **Connecting with Past Learning:** Chapter 12, Section 3—discussion of corrections

PLANNING

Purpose: You may use this activity in combination with teacher-directed lessons for this chapter, as a performance-based assessment of content mastery, or as an enrichment project.

Suggested Time: Plan to spend five to seven 45-minute class periods on this project. Allow one class period to introduce the activity, hold a class discussion of the U.S. legal system, and assign student roles. Give groups two to three class periods to research teen courts. Set aside one or two class periods for students to hold a mock teen court trial. An additional class period should be used for the jury to reach a verdict and for the entire class to evaluate the outcome of the trial and discuss the effectiveness of teen courts.

Scale of Project: Students will need enough room to meet in groups and to hold a mock trial.

Group Size: Organize the class into seven groups of various sizes.

Materials: Students will need chairs and desks to simulate a courtroom, which should include a desk for the judge, a witness stand, a desk for the court reporter(s), one or two jury "boxes" with chairs, and separate tables for the prosecution and defense teams.

Resources: Have students use their textbooks, the Internet, the library, and any other materials that you provide to complete their research. If feasable, students may wish to contact attorneys or judges in your community to learn more about the legal system. Encourage students to explore and tap all available sources of information.

Preparation: Before starting the project, make copies of the Planning Guidelines and Project Task Sheets; you will need at least one copy for each group. You may also wish to make copies of the Standards for Evaluation form—which is a project-specific rubric—for students to use in preparing their presentations.

IMPLEMENTATION

1. Give students an overview of the activity by describing its four stages. Tell students that they will first discuss the nature and function of teen courts. They will then work in groups to research the purpose of teen courts and how they work. Next, students will participate in a mock teen court trial. Finally, students will discuss and evaluate the outcome of the trial and the effectiveness of teen courts.

2. To begin a discussion of teen courts, have students review Section 3 of Chapter 12, entitled "Corrections." Direct students' attention to the "Citizenship in Action" feature, entitled "Teen Court." Ask students to name the options available to judges when sentencing juveniles, and list them on the chalkboard. *(warning and dismissal, counseling, juvenile detention center, probation, community service, fines, boot camps, teen court)* Encourage students to evaluate whether teen court is a good alternative to juvenile courts.

3. Ensure that students understand the following terms: probation, juvenile delinquent, jury, deliberation, prosecution, defense, witness, and court reporter. It might be helpful to list the terms on the chalkboard and have the students define them.

4. Distribute copies of the Planning Guidelines and the Project Task Sheets. Go over the instructions on the Planning Guidelines to make sure that students understand the assignment. To have students choose roles, post the Project Task Sheets as sign-up sheets. You may wish to have two separate juries so that at the end of the exercise you can discuss the fact that different juries may reach different verdicts.

5. Have the groups begin researching teen courts. Each group should write a short description of the purpose and workings of teen courts in their state, if any, or teen courts in another state. They should also make a list of the possible punishments handed down by teen courts. Then, they should write a list of guidelines for their role in teen court. Judges should also prepare a list of questions they would like to ask witnesses and write instructions to the jury. Attorneys should make a list of questions to ask the witnesses and write opening and closing arguments to make to the court.

6. Once students have completed their research, set up the classroom to resemble a courtroom and have students take their places. The court reporter may open the trial by introducing the judge and the parties involved. The prosecution gives a five-minute opening statement, followed by the defense team's five-minute opening statement. The judge will then tell the prosecution to call its witnesses. The prosecution and defense teams have five minutes each to question both witnesses. The judge may ask questions of the witnesses. Then allow the defense team five minutes to make its final argument to the jury and the prosecution the same amount of time to make its closing argument.

7. Once final arguments are complete, the judge should instruct the jury that it will now meet privately to decide the defendant's guilt and punishment. Have the judge tell the jury that their decision must be unanimous. The jury should have at least 30 minutes to make its decision. After jury members have reached a verdict, have them write down their decision. Then have the judge read the verdict aloud.

8. End the activity with a class discussion about the verdict and the effectiveness of teen courts in general. Following the discussion, have students write a short evaluation of how important their role was in teen court and explain their reasons why they think the verdict(s) was fair or not fair.

ASSESSMENT

1. Use the Standards for Evaluation form to help you evaluate students' work in researching and simulating a teen court trial.

2. An option for additional individual assessment is to grade student's written description of teen court and the guidelines and analysis of their role in the simulation.

3. Alternatively, you can assess student performance by using any or all of the following rubrics from the *Alternative Assessment Handbook* on the *One-Stop Planner CD-ROM:* Rubric 1: Acquiring Information, Rubric 11: Discussions, Rubric 12: Drawing Conclusions, Rubric 14: Group Activity, Rubric 16: Judging Information, Rubric 30: Research.

PLANNING GUIDELINES

One of your fellow students has been accused of committing a misdemeanor crime: vandalizing school lockers with spray paint. The juvenile court judge has referred the case to a teen court made up of you and other students. Your job is to participate in a mock trial to determine whether the accused student is guilty or innocent. If guilty, the trial will also decide the student's sentence.

You will be assigned one of the roles outlined in the following Project Task Sheets. Use available resources to research how teen courts work, what punishments they hand out, and the responsibilities of each role. After a verdict has been reached, the class will discuss the effectiveness of teen courts, so be prepared to analyze the court proceedings.

PROJECT TASK SHEET

The Judge: Your role is to preside over the mock trial, ask attorneys or witnesses any questions you think might help the jury make a decision, and to answer any questions the jury may have. Tell the jury that they must reach a unanimous decision. Once the jury has reached a decision, you will read the jury's decision, or verdict, to the court.

(1) _____   (2) _____

PROJECT TASK SHEET

Court Reporter: Your job is to open the court proceedings and to take notes during the trial. You should write down every word spoken in court.

(1) _____   (2) _____

PROJECT TASK SHEET

Prosecution Team: Your role is to convince the jury that the defendant is guilty and that they should hand down the maximum sentence. You will make a five-minute opening statement, question each witness for up to five minutes, and summarize your case in a five-minute closing argument. Assign each task to a team member.

(1) _____   (3) _____
(2) _____   (4) _____

PROJECT TASK SHEET

Defense Team: Your role is to convince the jury that the defendant is innocent. You will make a five-minute opening statement to present your case, question each witness for up to five minutes, and summarize your case in a five-minute closing argument. Assign each task to a team member.

(1) _____   (3) _____
(2) _____   (4) _____

PROJECT TASK SHEET

Witness for the Prosecution: You are the prosecution's star witness. You did not actually see the student vandalize the lockers, but you saw the defendant near the lockers around the time the vandalism occurred. You also noticed some paint on the defendant's shirt.

(1) _____

PROJECT TASK SHEET

Witness for the Defense: You are the defense team's star witness. You did not actually see the student vandalize the lockers, but you saw the defendant talking to an older student near the lockers around the time the vandalism occurred. You think the older student was forcing the defendant to vandalize the locker of a fellow student.

(1) _____

PROJECT TASK SHEET

Jury: It is your responsibility to listen to all of the evidence presented in court, decide whether the defendant is guilty or innocent, and decide the punishment, if any. You may ask the judge questions during the trial. You must reach a unanimous decision about the defendant's guilt or innocence. Once this decision is reached, write your decision and hand it to the judge. You may wish to elect a jury foreperson to lead the discussion and be the spokesperson for the jury.

Jury 1	Jury 2
(1) _____	(1) _____
(2) _____	(2) _____
(3) _____	(3) _____
(4) _____	(4) _____

STANDARDS FOR EVALUATION

EXCELLENT

- The student's research shows a thorough understanding of the purpose and workings of teen court.
- The student's participation in the mock trial shows a thorough understanding of his or her assigned role.
- The student participates fully in the mock trial and class discussion.

GOOD

- The student's research shows a good understanding of the purpose and workings of teen court.
- The student's participation in the mock trial shows a good understanding of his or her assigned role.
- The student participates fully in the mock trial and class discussion.

ACCEPTABLE

- The student's research shows a basic understanding of the purpose and workings of teen court.
- The student's participation in the mock trial shows a basic understanding of his or her assigned role.
- The student participates in the mock trial and class discussion.

UNACCEPTABLE

- The student's research does not show an understanding of the purpose and workings of teen court.
- The student's participation in the mock trial fails to show an understanding of his or her assigned role.
- The student does not participate fully in the mock trial and class discussion.

THE FIRST AMENDMENT AND YOU: RIGHTS AND RESPONSIBILITIES

GOAL

In this activity students will learn about the First Amendment of the Constitution by producing a student handbook on their rights and responsibilities related to religious expression, speech, and assembly and petition.

OVERVIEW

This project has four components: group discussion, research, creation of a student handbook, and response to the finalized student handbook. First, students will participate in a discussion about First Amendment rights and responsibilities. Then student groups will research how these rights apply to them at school and analyze recent Supreme Court cases relating to First Amendment rights. Next, students will prepare a student handbook that details their First Amendment rights and responsibilities. Finally, the student handbook will be evaluated by school administrators, by civil liberties experts, or by a group of student peers.

OBJECTIVES

After completing this activity, students will be able to:

- describe First Amendment freedoms of religion, speech, and assembly and petition;
- identify limitations on First Amendment freedoms;
- explain how First Amendment freedoms apply to high school students;
- locate Supreme Court decisions relating to First Amendment freedoms;
- analyze Supreme Court decisions relating to First Amendment freedoms;
- apply Supreme Court decisions to everyday life;
- identify responsibilities that go hand-in-hand with First Amendment freedoms.

LEARNING CONNECTIONS

- Learning Styles: interpersonal, linguistic, visual-spatial

- Skills Mastery: acquiring information, defining/clarifying problems, determining the strength of an argument, drawing conclusions, judging information, navigating the Internet, solving problems, synthesizing information, writing mastery: informing
- ***Connecting with Past Learning:*** Chapter 2, Section 5—discussion of the debate over a bill of rights; Chapter 3, Section 2—discussion of the Bill of Rights; Chapter 11, Section 2—discussion of the workings of the Supreme Court; Chapter 13, Sections 1 through 4—discussion of civil liberties and freedoms of religion, speech, assembly, and petition

PLANNING

Purpose: You may use this activity in combination with teacher-directed lessons for this chapter, as a performance-based assessment of content mastery, or as an enrichment project.

Suggested Time: Plan to spend about six to eight 45-minute class periods on this project. Allow one class period to hold a group discussion about First Amendment freedoms and responsibilities, introduce the activity, and organize groups. Give student groups two or three class periods to research their section of the student handbook. Then allow two or three class periods for individual groups to discuss their research findings and prepare their sections of the student handbook. Once the individual sections of the student handbook are finalized and the completed handbook is ready, allow one class period for a school administrator, civil liberties expert, or peer review committee to discuss the student handbook with the class.

Scale of Project: You will need enough room for students to work together in groups and for guests to present evaluations of the finalized student handbook.

Group Size: Organize the class into three groups. Each group will research and prepare one section of the student handbook.

Materials: Students will need paper and access to a typewriter or word processor to produce the final student handbook.

Resources: Have students use their textbooks, the Internet, the library, and any other materials that you provide to complete their research. Several World Wide Web sites are particularly useful for this project. The American Civil Liberties Web site (http://www.aclu.org/issues/student/hmes.html) examines student rights. In addition, Cornell Law Library provides a searchable archive of Supreme Court cases (http://supct.law.cornell.edu/supct/). If feasible, students might also wish to contact civil rights attorneys or local judges working in your community. Encourage students to explore and tap all available sources of information.

Preparation: Before starting the project, make copies of the Planning Guidelines and Project Task Sheet; you will need at least one copy for each group. You may also wish to make copies of the Standards for Evaluation form—which is a project-specific rubric—for students to use in preparing their student handbook.

IMPLEMENTATION

1. Give students an overview of the activity by describing its four stages. Tell students that they will first discuss their First Amendment rights on campus and the responsibilities that go along with First Amendment rights. They will then research Supreme Court and other legal decisions related to these rights and responsibilities. Next, students will combine their research into a handbook of rights and responsibilities for students in their school. Then, a school administrator, legal expert, or peer-review panel will evaluate the handbook.

2. To begin the discussion of First Amendment rights, write the following three headings on the chalkboard: *Religion, Speech,* and *Assembly and Petition.* Ask students to give examples of these First Amendment rights that they have at school. *(Examples might include religious clubs, school newspaper stories, and student petitions for changes in the cafeteria menu.)* As you write student responses on the chalkboard, challenge students to analyze how these activities relate to the First Amendment. Then ask students to explain what responsibilities go along with these rights. *(Examples might include showing respect for the opinions of*

other people and for different religions, pursuing nonlibelous, fair, and impartial reporting in the school newspaper, avoiding bigoted expressions, not disrupting other students' learning experience.)

3. Ensure that students understand the following terms: civil liberty, Establishment Clause, Free Exercise Clause, treason, libel, slander, obscenity, symbolic speech, hate speech, and picketing. If necessary, have students use the Glossary at the back of the textbook to write the definitions of these terms.

4. Assign or have students form into three groups. Each group will research and present one section of the student handbook. Distribute copies of the Planning Guidelines and Project Task Sheet to each group. Go over the instructions to make sure that students understand the assignment. Before groups begin their research, encourage group members to brainstorm about and list rules for acceptable and unacceptable speech, behaviors, or religious activities. Have them give their opinion of whether these rules would comply with the First Amendment. If you wish, also distribute copies of the Standards for Evaluation form at this time.

5. Have student groups begin researching recent court cases and controversies involving First Amendment rights in the public schools. Guide students in breaking down the research into manageable portions. Some students might track down historical and contemporary Supreme Court cases, while other students might concentrate their research on locating lower-level court decisions. Still other students might focus on First Amendment controversies that were settled outside of the courts. Tell students to write a short synopsis of each court case or controversy they research.

6. When the students have completed their research, have the individual groups meet to analyze their findings. Groups should evaluate whether the lists of rules they developed in their brainstorming sessions are in line with Supreme Court and lower court decisions. Each group should then apply these decisions to write out guidelines for acceptable and unacceptable conduct for members of the school community. Remind students that these guidelines should list student responsibilities as well as rights and freedoms.

7. After all groups have completed their sections of the student handbook, have the class vote on an appropriate title for the handbook. Then have students combine the various sections into a finished handbook with a titled cover, and distribute it to the class. To evaluate the results, ask a school administrator, legal expert, or student group to meet with the class to comment on and discuss the student handbook.

ASSESSMENT

1. Use the Standards for Evaluation form to help you evaluate student participation in creating the student handbook.

2. Individual grades can be based on the handbook section produced by the group.

3. An option for additional individual assessment is to grade student synopses of the court cases and controversies they researched.

4. Alternatively, you can assess student performance by using any or all of the following rubrics from the *Alternative Assessment Handbook* on the *One-Stop Planner CD-ROM:* Rubric 1: Acquiring Information, Rubric 11: Discussions, Rubric 12: Drawing Conclusions, Rubric 14: Group Activity, Rubric 16: Judging Information, Rubric 30: Research, Rubric 38: Writing to Classify, Rubric 40: Writing to Describe, Rubric 42: Writing to Inform.

PLANNING GUIDELINES

"First Amendment rights, applied in light of the special characteristics of the school environment, are available to teachers and students. It can hardly be argued that either students or teachers shed their constitutional rights to freedom of speech or expression at the schoolhouse gate. This has been the unmistakable holding of this Court for almost 50 years."

—*Tinker* v. *Des Moines* (1969)

In 1969 the Supreme Court spelled out students' right to free speech in *Tinker* v. *Des Moines.* This important decision, however, acknowledged the "special characteristics of the school environment." When exercising their free speech rights, students cannot be "disruptive" or "impinge upon the rights of others." In other words, the right to free speech comes with important responsibilities to the rest of the school community.

Your class's assignment is to create a student handbook that details students' First Amendment rights and responsibilities. The handbook will be divided into three sections: "Religion in Our School," "Free Speech on Campus," and "Your Rights of Assembly and Petition." The student handbook will be based on the First Amendment rights outlined in Supreme Court decisions, federal and state court cases, and recent controversies in the news. The handbook should provide rules about such First Amendment issues as free speech in your student newspaper, prayer and religion-oriented student groups in school, hate speech, and acceptable and unacceptable forms of student protest.

PROJECT TASK SHEET

Section 1: Religion in Our School
Your group's assignment is to locate and analyze Supreme Court, federal court, and state court cases and news stories that focus on freedom of religion issues in the public schools. Each student will write a brief synopsis of one such court case or controversy. Use the synopses to write guidelines for religion in your school. Divide these guidelines into "What You Can Do," "What You Cannot Do," and "Your Responsibilities."

Section 2: Free Speech on Campus
Your group's assignment is to locate and analyze Supreme Court, federal court, and state court cases and news stories that focus on freedom of speech issues in the public schools. Each student will write a brief synopsis of one such court case or controversy. Use the synopses to write guidelines for free speech in your school. Divide these guidelines into "What You Can Say," "What You Cannot Say," and "Your Responsibilities."

Section 3: Your Rights of Assembly and Petition
Your group's assignment is to locate and analyze Supreme Court, federal court, and state court cases and news stories that focus on freedom of assembly and petition issues in the public schools. Each student will write a brief synopsis of one such court case or controversy. Use the synopses to write guidelines for student protests in your school. Divide these guidelines into "What You Can Do," "What You Cannot Do," and "Your Responsibilities."

STANDARDS FOR EVALUATION

EXCELLENT

- The group demonstrates a thorough knowledge of First Amendment rights and responsibilities.
- The group finds more than two appropriate First Amendment court cases and controversies and fully analyzes and applies them to their school.
- All group members contribute fully to the research, discussion, and writing of the student handbook.

GOOD

- The group demonstrates a satisfactory knowledge of First Amendment rights and responsibilities.
- The group finds at least two appropriate First Amendment court cases and controversies and analyzes and applies them to their school.
- All group members contribute to the research, discussion, and writing of the student handbook.

ACCEPTABLE

- The group demonstrates some knowledge of First Amendment rights and responsibilities.
- The group finds two appropriate First Amendment court cases and controversies and explains them.
- Most group members contribute to the research, discussion, and writing of the student handbook.

UNACCEPTABLE

- The group demonstrates little knowledge of First Amendment rights and responsibilities.
- The group's First Amendment court cases and controversies are not applicable to a public school environment.
- Few group members contribute to the research, discussion, and writing of the student handbook.

└─ "DEATH ROW DAYS"—A SPECIAL REPORT

GOAL

In this activity students will learn about the controversies surrounding the issue of capital punishment by producing a *Nightline*-style investigative television news program.

OVERVIEW

This project has four components: group discussion, research, script writing, and filming or presentation of project segments. First, students will participate in a discussion about capital punishment. Then student groups will research the death penalty, focusing on its history, statistics, court cases, controversies, and expert opinions. Next, student groups will write and produce segments of the investigative television news report based on their research, including a final segment with a town hall meeting to air the class's views on capital punishment.

OBJECTIVES

After completing this activity, students will be able to:
- explain what capital punishment is;
- identify states in which capital punishment is allowed;
- identify the number of capital executions that occur in a given year;
- summarize the history of the death penalty as a punishment for major crimes;
- identify major court cases relating to capital punishment;
- prepare charts and other graphics containing statistical information on capital punishment;
- discuss the arguments for and against capital punishment;
- evaluate the effectiveness of capital punishment as a deterrent to crime;
- organize a debate;
- debate a controversial issue;
- write an effective script;
- analyze the components of a successful news program;
- produce a segment of a news program;
- hold a town hall meeting;
- appreciate the importance of airing conflicting views.

LEARNING CONNECTIONS

- Learning Styles: interpersonal, intrapersonal, linguistic, visual-spatial
- Skills Mastery: acquiring information, debating ideas, determining the strength of an argument, distinguishing fact and opinion, judging information, making comparisons, navigating the Internet, presenting data graphically, recognizing point of view, synthesizing information, understanding cause and effect, writing mastery: creating, writing mastery: informing
- ***Connecting with Past Learning:*** Chapter 3, Section 2—chart showing Eighth Amendment's prohibition against cruel and unusual punishment; Chapter 12, Section 3—discussion of capital punishment; Chapter 14, Section 3—discussion of capital punishment

PLANNING

Purpose: You may use this activity in combination with teacher-directed lessons for this chapter, as a performance-based assessment of content mastery, or as an enrichment project.

Suggested Time: Plan to spend about nine to ten 45-minute class periods on this project. Allow one class period to hold a group discussion about the nature of capital punishment, introduce the activity, and organize student groups. Give students two class periods to research their segments of the television report. Allow three class periods to write and practice scripts. Instruct students to memorize their scripts at home. Allow three or four class periods for students to film or present their shows.

Scale of Project: You will need enough room for a television and videocassette recorder (VCR) in the front of the classroom. If students do not have access to the appropriate technology, they will need enough space to present their segments live in front of the class.

Group Size: Organize students into four groups of at least six students. Each group will research, write a script for, and produce a segment of a television investigative report on the death penalty. The members of each group should work cooperatively to fulfill all of their required tasks.

Materials: If students have access to technology, they will need a video camera to film their segments of the report and a television and videocassette recorder (VCR) to view the completed investigative news program. The students also may need name tags to distinguish the "experts" on the capital punishment panels. If possible, allow students to view a segment or two of the *Nightline* television program to help them understand the assignment.

Resources: Have students use their textbooks, the Internet, the library, and any other materials that you provide to complete their research. If feasible, students may wish to interview or correspond with experts from human rights organizations, such as Amnesty International, criminal lawyers, religious leaders, criminal justice professors, members of victim's rights groups, and corrections officials to compile a variety of opposing opinions about the death penalty. Encourage students to explore and tap all available sources of information.

Preparation: Before starting the project, make copies of the Planning Guidelines and Project Task Sheet; you will need at least one copy for each group. You may also wish to make copies of the Standards for Evaluation form—which is a project-specific rubric—for students to use in preparing their news report segments

IMPLEMENTATION

1. Give students an overview of the activity by describing its four stages. Tell students that they will first discuss capital punishment. They will then work with their groups to research various aspects of the capital punishment issue. Next, student groups will use their research to write and produce four segments of an investigative news report, including a final town hall meeting to survey student attitudes about the death penalty.

2. To begin the discussion of capital punishment, refer students to the map of the United States on textbook page 333, entitled "States That Allow the Death Penalty." Ask students to determine whether their state allows the death penalty. Challenge students to explain why some states allow the death penalty and others do not.

3. Ensure that students understand the following terms: Eighth Amendment, cruel and unusual punishment, capital punishment, death penalty, and deterrent. If necessary, have students use the Glossary at the back of the textbook or a dictionary to write the definitions of these terms.

4. Organize the class into four groups. Distribute copies of the Planning Guidelines and Project Task Sheet and, if you wish, copies of the Standards for Evaluation form. Go over the instructions on the Planning Guidelines to make sure that students understand the assignment. Either assign or have each group choose a television news segment to research and film or present. If the groups choose their own segments, act as the new report's director and circulate among the class to make sure that there is no overlap. If possible, screen a segment or two from the television news program *Nightline* for the class to view and critique. Encourage students to come up with a title for their news program.

5. Before the student groups begin their research, guide the groups in assigning roles as producers, news anchors, writers, and "experts" on the death penalty. If necessary, offer clarification on the nature and substance of these roles as they pertain to the television industry. Have student groups begin researching their segment of the television show on capital punishment. If feasible, students may wish to interview actual legal experts for the background segments of their shows. Students who play the role of death-penalty experts can use these interviews in preparing their interview responses.

6. Once students have completed their research, have the groups meet to write their script, which should include an introductory sequence, a summary of the issue, a 5- to 10-minute background segment, expert interviews, and concluding remarks. Guide the groups in producing graphs, charts, and additional graphics to illustrate their shows. Groups should make sure that they have enough information to produce a 30-minute television news report. Encourage students to rehearse their script before "air-time."

7. After the groups have completed and rehearsed their scripts, have students film the first three shows. Then have the class view the first three shows, and conduct a class discussion after each show. Encourage students to write a short review of the shows from the perspective of a journalist familiar with the issue of capital punishment. After screening the first three shows, film the "Town Hall Meeting" show. Have the students who are not a part of the group producing the show serve as audience members for the Town Hall Meeting. If students do not have access to video technology, have them present their shows live in front of the class.

ASSESSMENT

1. Use the Standards for Evaluation form to help you evaluate student participation in creating the television news program.

2. Individual grades can be based on the segment of the program worked on by the student.

3. An option for additional individual assessment is to grade student reviews of the television news program.

4. Alternatively, you can assess student performance by using any or all of the following rubrics from the *Alternative Assessment Handbook* on the *One-Stop Planner CD-ROM:* Rubric 1: Acquiring Information, Rubric 7: Charts, Rubric 10: Debates, Rubric 11: Discussions, Rubric 14: Group Activity, Rubric 16: Judging Information, Rubric 22: Multimedia Presentations, Rubric 29: Presentations, Rubric 30: Research, Rubric 33: Skits and Reader's Theater, Rubric 39: Writing to Create, Rubric 42: Writing to Inform.

PLANNING GUIDELINES

The president of the HSBC (High School Broadcasting Corporation) network wants to present a hard-hitting investigative report on capital punishment. As part of the crew of HSBC's late-night investigative news program, your assignment is to produce one show in the four-part series on capital punishment.

The first three shows will each consist of the following segments and roles to play:
- **Segment 1:** Introductory sequence: title, music, images from show (1 or 2 producers)
- **Segment 2:** Short introduction to show (News anchor)
- **Segment 3:** A 5- to 10-minute background segment (2 or 3 producers and writers)
- **Segment 4:** Interview/debate (News anchor interviews 2 capital punishment "experts")
- **Segment 5:** Concluding remarks (News anchor)

The fourth show will include a "Town Hall Meeting" for class members to air their views on the death penalty. It will include the following segments and roles:
- **Segment 1:** Introductory sequence: title, music, images from show (1 or 2 producers)
- **Segment 2:** Short introduction to show (News anchor)
- **Segment 3:** A 5- to 10-minute background segment (2 or 3 producers and writers)
- **Segment 4:** Town hall panel/discussion (Audience members, news anchor, 2 experts)
- **Segment 5:** Concluding remarks (News anchor)

PROJECT TASK SHEET

First Show: Crime and Punishment
Dramatize the issue of the death penalty by focusing on a real death-row case. Present the people and chronology of the court case, appeals, and execution. The news anchor should interview at least two experts: one opposed to the punishment in this case and another in favor of it.

Second Show: History of Capital Punishment
Present the history of capital punishment in the United States. The news anchor should interview at least two experts: a legal historian opposed to capital punishment and another in favor of it.

Third Show: Capital Punishment Around the World
Describe where and how the death penalty is practiced around the world. The news anchor should interview at least two experts: a representative of an international human rights organization opposed to capital punishment and a foreign lawyer, jurist, or politician who supports capital punishment.

Fourth Show: Capital Punishment—A Deterrent to Crime?
Present statistics and expert opinions on whether the death penalty has a deterrent effect on crime. The news anchor should interview at least two experts: a criminal justice professor who opposes the death penalty and a prison official who favors it.

STANDARDS FOR EVALUATION

EXCELLENT

- The group demonstrates a thorough knowledge of the issues surrounding capital punishment.
- The group presents a balanced, in-depth, and clear exploration of opposing sides of the capital punishment issue.
- All group members contribute fully to the research, writing, and production of their show.

GOOD

- The group demonstrates an adequate knowledge of the issues surrounding capital punishment.
- The group presents a clear, balanced exploration of opposing sides of the capital punishment issue.
- All group members contribute to the research, writing, and production of their show.

ACCEPTABLE

- The group demonstrates some knowledge of the issues surrounding capital punishment.
- The group introduces opposing sides of the capital punishment issue.
- Most group members contribute to the research, writing, and production of their show.

UNACCEPTABLE

- The group demonstrates little knowledge of the issues surrounding capital punishment.
- The group explores only one side of the capital punishment issue.
- Few group members contribute to the research, writing, and production of their show.

BATTLES FOUGHT WITH WORDS: A CIVIL RIGHTS MUSEUM

GOAL

In this activity students will learn about the importance of Supreme Court cases in winning civil rights for African Americans by preparing a Civil Rights Museum exhibit.

OVERVIEW

This project has four components: group discussion, research, preparation of exhibits, and a "tour" of the museum. First, students will participate in a discussion about Supreme Court cases that have focused on civil rights issues. Then student groups will research a particular Supreme Court case. Next, student groups will prepare a museum exhibit on their assigned case. Finally, groups will conduct a tour of the completed "museum" for the class or other interested groups.

OBJECTIVES

After completing this activity, students will be able to:
- explain the role of the courts in ensuring civil rights for all Americans;
- recognize the importance of the Fourteenth Amendment's Equal Protection Clause;
- evaluate the social effects of important civil rights cases;
- summarize the events leading up to important civil rights cases;
- identify the people involved in major civil rights cases;
- analyze the legal arguments presented in major civil rights cases;
- produce a museum exhibit;
- produce visual and other materials that effectively convey information.

LEARNING CONNECTIONS

- Learning Styles: body-kinesthetic, interpersonal, linguistic, visual-spatial
- Skills Mastery: acquiring information, creating time lines, defining/clarifying problems, determining the strength of an argument, drawing

conclusions, judging information, navigating the Internet, recognizing point of view, solving problems, synthesizing information, understanding cause and effect, writing mastery: informing

- *Connecting with Past Learning:* Chapter 1, Section 1—discussion of the government's role in promoting values; Chapter 3, Section 2—discussion of the Thirteenth, Fourteenth, and Fifteenth Amendments; Chapter 11, Section 1—role of the courts; Chapter 11, Section 2 and Section 3—discussion of *Brown v. Board of Education of Topeka;* Chapter 15, Section 2—discussion of the diversity of the United States; Chapter 15, Section 3 and Section 4—discussion of the struggle for civil rights and discussion of civil rights laws

PLANNING

Purpose: You may use this activity in combination with teacher-directed lessons for this chapter, as a performance-based assessment of content mastery, or as an enrichment project.

Suggested Time: Plan to spend about six to eight 45-minute class periods on this project. Allow one class period to hold a group discussion about civil rights, introduce the activity, and organize groups. Give students two or three class periods to research their exhibits. Allow two or three class periods for groups to prepare their exhibits. Use a final class period to evaluate the exhibits by hosting a "tour" for the class or other groups.

Scale of Project: Students will need enough room to present and view their exhibits. If possible, arrange for the exhibits to be displayed in a public viewing area of your school.

Group Size: Organize the class into six groups. Each group will research a Supreme Court case that focused on a civil rights issue and prepare an exhibit for the civil rights museum.

Materials: Students may use a wide range of materials for their exhibits. They made need poster board and other art materials to produce displays. Felt-covered wooden panels can be used to display the exhibits. Students may also use more high-tech materials, including videotapes, audiotapes, or computers, in their exhibits.

Resources: Have students use their textbooks, the Internet, the library, and any other materials that you provide to complete their research. Several World Wide Web sites provide transcripts of Supreme Court decisions that students may use in their exhibits. Students may also wish to contact attorneys or court judges in your community to learn more about constitutional issues surrounding the protection of civil rights. Encourage students to explore and tap all available sources of information.

Preparation: Before starting the project, make copies of the Planning Guidelines and Project Task Sheet; you will need at least one copy for each group. You may also wish to make copies of the Standards for Evaluation form—which is a project-specific rubric—for students to use in preparing their museum exhibits.

IMPLEMENTATION

1. Give students an overview of the activity by describing its four stages. Tell students that they will first discuss how the courts have extended civil rights to African Americans. Student groups will then research the people, events, and legal arguments of an important civil rights Supreme Court case. Next, student groups will use their research findings to prepare an exhibit for a "Civil Rights Museum." They will then conduct a tour of the museum to present their exhibits.

2. To begin the discussion of civil rights Supreme Court cases, have students review the Section 3 Summary found at the end of Chapter 15. Ask students to explain how federal courts decide whether distinctions between groups of people are valid. *(They use the rational basis test and strict scrutiny test.)* Challenge students to explain and give examples of why Supreme Court cases are sometimes needed to ensure Americans' civil rights. *(State laws and social standards vary and do not always follow the Fourteenth Amendment's Equal Protection Clause, i.e., Jim Crow laws, de jure segregation, and so on.)*

3. Ensure that students understand the following terms: civil rights, suspect classification, civil rights movement, segregation, Jim Crow law, *de jure* segregation, separate-but-equal doctrine, *de facto* segregation, affirmative action, and quota. If necessary, have students use the Glossary at the back of the textbook or a dictionary to write the definitions of these terms.

4. Organize the class into six groups. Assign or have each group choose a Supreme Court case to research. Distribute copies of the Planning Guidelines and Project Task Sheet to each group and, if you wish, copies of the Standards for Evaluation form. Go over the instructions on the Planning Guidelines to make sure that students understand the assignment. Have students discuss museum exhibits they have seen and enjoyed. Encourage the student groups to make lists of things that have been included in effective exhibits, such as text or quotations to explain the exhibit, photographs of relevant individuals or groups, videotapes, recordings of speeches, recreations of historical scenes, hands-on type of activities, and costumes or other props.

5. Next, have student groups brainstorm about possible sources of information for their topic in addition to the textbook. Encourage students to explore a wide range of primary sources to recreate the time period, people, and issues surrounding their Supreme Court case, including letters, photographs, newspaper or magazine articles, biographies, interviews with civil rights activists and others concerned with the case, and written and oral transcripts of Supreme Court cases. Have each student locate a unique primary source and write a short report on what this sort of primary source can and cannot tell us about the Supreme Court case.

6. Once students have completed their research, have the groups meet to prepare their exhibits, which should include an overview of the Supreme Court case, a time line of the case, biographies of the significant individuals involved in the case, a summary of the legal arguments used to win the case, and information on the legal and social effects of the Supreme Court's decision. Encourage students to use a variety of media to prepare their exhibits.

7. After the groups have completed their exhibits, have students display them in a designated area. You might want to have students come up with a name and banner or sign for their

"museum" and exhibit. Have students each take part in leading a tour of the exhibit, showing how their individual contributions to the exhibit illustrate the Supreme Court cases. You might wish to invite students and teachers from other classes or schools to tour the civil rights museum. Create a bulletin board so that students and teachers can express their reactions to the exhibit.

ASSESSMENT

1. Use the Standards for Evaluation form to help you evaluate the exhibits.

2. Individual grades can be based on the student's written evaluation of primary source materials.

3. An option for additional individual assessment is to grade student tour guides' presentations.

4. Alternatively, you can assess student performance by using any or all of the following rubrics from the *Alternative Assessment Handbook* on the *One-Stop Planner CD-ROM:* Rubric 1: Acquiring Information, Rubric 3: Artwork, Rubric 4: Biographies, Rubric 6: Cause and Effect, Rubric 14: Group Activity, Rubric 16: Judging Information, Rubric 22: Multimedia Presentations, Rubric 29: Presentations, Rubric 30: Research, Rubric 34: Slogans and Banners, Rubric 36: Time Lines, Rubric 42: Writing to Inform.

PLANNING GUIDELINES

White and black Freedom Riders rode buses throughout the South challenging segregation. Young African American protesters staged sit-ins at lunch counters. Hundreds of thousands of people marched on Washington to demand justice for African Americans. These were just some of the dramatic—and sometimes dangerous—ways that people waged the campaign for civil rights.

Yet some of the civil rights gains were made in a less dramatic fashion. Lawyers—including Thurgood Marshall, who later went on to become the first African American Supreme Court justice—constructed elegant legal arguments to challenge in the courts all forms of segregation in U.S. society. Some court cases even upheld the right to take part in the sit-ins and Freedom Rides that were so crucial to the civil rights movement.

To recognize the civil rights gains won through the courts, design an exhibit for a Civil Rights Museum. Each of the six exhibits should provide an overview of an important Supreme Court case, a time line of the case, biographies of the lawyers and plaintiffs involved, a summary of the legal arguments used to win the case, and information on the legal and social effects of the decision.

PROJECT TASK SHEET

Choose one of the cases below that helped African Americans secure the basic civil rights guaranteed to all Americans.

- *Sweatt* v. *Painter* (1950): desegregated the University of Texas law school

- *Brown* v. *Board of Education of Topeka* (1954): outlawed segregation in the public schools

- *Garner* v. *Louisiana* (1961): upheld the right to stage peaceful sit-ins

- *Bailey* v. *Patterson* (1963): filed on behalf of Freedom Riders; ruled against segregation in interstate travel

- *Heart of Atlanta Motel, Inc.* v. *United States* (1964): upheld the validity of the Civil Rights Act of 1964, which outlawed discrimination in hotels and motels

- *Shuttlesworth* v. *City of Birmingham* (1969): ruled unconstitutional a parade ordinance that prevented civil rights leaders from getting permission to hold marches

STANDARDS FOR EVALUATION

EXCELLENT

- The exhibit reflects a thorough, in-depth knowledge of the people, events, and effects of the civil rights Supreme Court case.
- The display includes a wide range of primary sources that effectively explain the Supreme Court case.
- All group members contribute fully to the research, production, and presentation of the civil rights museum exhibit.

GOOD

- The exhibit reflects a good knowledge of the people, events, and effects of the civil rights Supreme Court case.
- The display includes several primary sources that effectively explain the Supreme Court case.
- All group members contribute to the research, production, and presentation of the civil rights museum exhibit.

ACCEPTABLE

- The exhibit reflects some knowledge of the people, events, and effects of the civil rights Supreme Court case.
- The display includes at least two kinds of primary sources that explain the Supreme Court case.
- Most group members contribute to the research, production, and presentation of the civil rights museum exhibit.

UNACCEPTABLE

- The exhibit demonstrates little knowledge of the people, events, and effects of the civil rights Supreme Court case.
- The display includes fewer than two primary sources relating to the Supreme Court case.
- Few group members contribute to the research, production, and presentation of the civil rights museum exhibit.

WHAT'S ON THE NEWS?: A MEDIA SURVEY

GOAL

In this activity students will learn about how effectively the media carries out its main functions by surveying one week of radio, television, newspaper, magazine, and Internet news.

OVERVIEW

This project has six components: class discussion, writing survey questions, media observation, summarizing results, presentation of results, and class discussion and comparison of results. First, students will participate in a class discussion of the media's responsibility to serve the public good. Then student groups will write survey questions to evaluate the media's effectiveness in providing news. Next, the student groups each will observe a particular medium for one week. In so doing, they will keep a log of the news programs they observe and write summaries of their observations. The groups will then meet to evaluate their findings and each write a summary of their results. Each group will present its evaluation to the class. Finally, the class as a whole will compare the evaluations and discuss whether the news media objectively and accurately reports important news.

OBJECTIVES

After completing this activity, students will be able to:
- identify the main functions of the media;
- identify the main types of media;
- write survey questions;
- make observations to complete a survey;
- evaluate the objectivity of the media;
- explain the role of the media in influencing public opinion;
- identify criticisms of the media;
- analyze the content of news programs;
- compile survey data to reach conclusions;
- compare and contrast the effectiveness of various medium's news programs.

LEARNING CONNECTIONS

- Learning Styles: interpersonal, linguistic
- Skills Mastery: acquiring information, distinguishing fact and opinion, drawing conclusions, judging information, making comparisons, navigating the Internet, recognizing point of view, synthesizing information, writing mastery: describing
- *Connecting with Past Learning:* Chapter 13, Section 3—discussion of freedom of the press; Chapter 16, Section 1—discussion of the influence of the media on public opinion; Chapter 16, Section 3—discussion of the media and the public good

PLANNING

Purpose: You may use this activity in combination with teacher-directed lessons for this chapter, as a performance-based assessment of content mastery, or as an enrichment project.

Suggested Time: Plan to spend about four to seven 45-minute class periods and one week of out-of-class observation time on this project. Allow one class period to hold a group discussion about the news media, introduce the activity, and organize groups. Give student groups one or two class periods to write their survey questions. Then allow one week for students to observe news programs outside of class. Give the groups one or two class periods to discuss their observations and prepare their written summaries. Once the summaries are completed, allow one or two class periods for groups to present their results and to hold a class discussion to compare the groups' observations.

Scale of Project: You will need enough room for students to work in groups and for the groups to present their summaries.

Group Size: Organize the class into four or five groups. Each group will observe one form of media, including radio, television, newspapers, magazines, and the Internet (optional).

Materials: Students will need access to radio, television, newspapers, magazines, and the Internet (optional). If students do not have access to these media at home, you may need to arrange for them to get access to these sources during class time or a study period. If feasible, students may also need access to a photocopy machine to make copies of their surveys.

Resources: Have students observe news programs on television, radio, and the Internet, and in newspapers and newsmagazines. If feasible, students may also wish to conduct journalism professors at colleges or universities in your community to learn more about the news media. Encourage students to explore and tap all available sources of information.

Preparation: Before starting the project, make copies of the Planning Guidelines and Project Task Sheet; you will need at least one copy for each group. You may also wish to make copies of the Standards for Evaluation form—which is a project-specific rubric—for students to use in preparing their media surveys.

IMPLEMENTATION

1. Give students an overview of the activity by describing its six stages. Tell students that they will first participate in a class discussion about the news media. They will then work in groups to write survey questions. Next, each student will observe one type of news presentation every day for one week, keeping a log of their observations and writing a summary. Then the groups each will write an analysis of the individual observations. Each group will then present its analysis to the class. Finally, the class as a whole will compare the groups' analyses and evaluate whether the news media effectively fulfills its main functions.

2. To begin the class discussion of the news media, ask students to review the Section 3 Summary found at the end of Chapter 16. Have students identify and explain the three main functions of the media. *(informing the public, acting as gatekeeper, serving as watchdog)* As you write the students' responses on the chalkboard, challenge students to provide examples of these functions from each of the mediums

covered in this activity: radio, television, newspapers, newsmagazines, and the Internet (optional). Conclude the class discussion by asking students to identify some criticisms that have been leveled against the media. *(Criticisms include negative focus, bias, overreliance on visual images, and horse-race coverage.)*

3. Ensure that students understand the following terms: media, bias, objectivity, gatekeeper, watchdog, horse-race coverage, and survey. If necessary, have students use the Glossary at the back of the textbook or a dictionary to write the definitions of these terms.

4. Organize the class into four or five groups (depending on whether you wish to include the Internet among the media to be surveyed). Assign or have each group choose one of the following kinds of media: radio, television, newspapers, magazines, and the Internet (optional). Distribute copies of the Planning Guidelines and the Project Task Sheet to each group and, if you wish, copies of the Standards for Evaluation form. Go over the instructions on the Planning Guidelines to make sure that students understand the assignment.

5. Next, have student groups meet to write their survey questions. Point out that the survey questions should guide students in gathering the same information. You might want to circulate among the groups to make sure that students include in their surveys questions that cover the media's three main functions: informing the public, acting as gatekeeper, and serving as watchdog. Encourage students to write questions that critically examine whether their assigned news medium has an overall negative focus or political bias and whether it relies too much on visual images or horse-race coverage.

6. Once students have completed their surveys, have the groups compare their surveys. Groups may need to add questions to make the surveys more closely match each other. Then instruct students that they will have one week to observe a particular news medium. Stress that students should faithfully observe their news program every day for the assigned amount of time listed on their group's Project Task Sheet. Emphasize that their participation is crucial to creating a reliable survey. Tell students that they will be graded on the completeness of

their media logs and on the individual summaries of their observations.

7. After all groups have completed their observations, have the groups compile their individual summaries into a written evaluation of how effectively their assigned medium performs its three main functions. Encourage students to come up with a numerical scale to rank their assigned medium's effectiveness in each of these three areas.

8. Next, have students present their evaluations to the class. Each group can designate one student to present its findings. Alternatively, the presentation can be broken down into three segments, with each student evaluating one of the medium's functions. Groups may present charts, radio or television clips, news-article collages, pictures, or any other evidence that illustrates their assigned medium's functions. Finally, hold a class discussion to compare how well the various media fulfill their three primary functions. You may also wish to use the results of the survey as the basis of a class discussion on the influence of the media on public opinion.

ASSESSMENT

1. Use the Standards for Evaluation form to help you evaluate student participation in the media survey.

2. Individual grades can be based on the student's media log or media summary.

3. Alternatively, you can assess student performance by using any or all of the following rubrics from the *Alternative Assessment Handbook* on the *One-Stop Planner CD-ROM:* Rubric 1: Acquiring Information, Rubric 7: Charts, Rubric 8: Collages, Rubric 9: Comparing and Contrasting, Rubric 11: Discussions, Rubric 12: Drawing Conclusions, Rubric 14: Group Activity, Rubric 16: Judging Information, Rubric 29: Presentations, Rubric 40: Writing to Describe.

PLANNING GUIDELINES

In an angry editorial, well-known conservative journalist Lash Limberg has leveled a number of criticisms at the mainstream media. Limberg claims that the media fail to report the news objectively. They emphasize negative stories rather than reporting on what is good about the nation, Limberg points out. Limberg also accuses other journalists of biased reporting in favor of liberal causes.

Another of the journalist's major concerns is the lack of content in news programs. Limberg criticizes print and television journalists for covering only those stories that have an exciting visual element and ignoring important, less visual topics. Limberg also faults the media's emphasis on "winners" and "losers," which shortchanges important issues. The journalist concludes that the media fail to carry out their main functions.

As a member of the media watchdog group, "Eye on the News," you are responsible for investigating whether or not Limberg's criticisms of the media are valid. Your media team will come up with a list of survey questions that analyze story content, amount of negative stories, political bias, and use of visual images and horse-race coverage of a particular medium. Each media team will be responsible for analyzing the news content of a particular medium for one week and for writing and presenting a final report.

PROJECT TASK SHEET

The Radio Team: Your media team will survey commercial and public radio stations' news programs. Each team member will listen to one station's news programs for at least 30 minutes a day for one week. Keep a log of the content of each day's news program and write a one-page summary of your observations.

The Television Team: Your media team is responsible for surveying commercial and public television stations' news programs. Each team member will choose one station and watch its news program for at least 30 minutes a day for one week. Keep a log of the content of each day's news program and then write a one-page summary of your observations.

The Newspaper Team: Your media team is responsible for surveying local and national newspapers. Each team member will choose one newspaper and analyze its front-section news stories for one week. Keep a log of the content of each day's news stories and then write a one-page summary of your observations.

The Newsmagazine Team: Your media team is responsible for surveying weekly newsmagazines. Each team member will choose one issue of a different newsmagazine and analyze its news stories. Keep a log of the major news stories and then write a one-page summary of your observations.

The Internet Team: Your media team is responsible for surveying Internet news programs. Each team member will choose a different program and survey its news content for one week. Keep a log of the content of each day's news program and then write a one-page summary of your observations.

STANDARDS FOR EVALUATION

EXCELLENT

- The group's survey questions thoroughly analyze the medium's effectiveness in carrying out its functions and fully investigate the common criticisms of the media.
- The student's daily log and news summary show a thorough and careful analysis of the news content of his or her assigned medium.
- All group members participate fully in the media observations and final report.

GOOD

- The group's survey questions effectively analyze the medium's effectiveness in carrying out its functions and adequately investigate the common criticisms of the media.
- The student's daily log and news summary show a careful analysis of the news content of his or her assigned medium.
- All group members participate in the media observations and final report.

ACCEPTABLE

- The group's survey questions analyze the medium's effectiveness in carrying out its functions and investigate the common criticisms of the media.
- The student's daily log and news summary show a basic analysis of the news content of his or her assigned medium.
- Most group members participate in the media observations and final report.

UNACCEPTABLE

- The group's survey questions fail to analyze the medium's effectiveness in carrying out its functions or investigate the common criticisms of the media.
- The student's daily log and news summary fail to analyze the news content of his or her assigned medium.
- Fewer than half of the group members participate in the media observations and final report.

SAVE OUR SCHOOL: A LOBBYING CAMPAIGN

GOAL

In this activity students will learn about how interest groups influence public policy by organizing their own lobbying campaign.

OVERVIEW

This project has six components: class discussion, group planning session, research, preparation of lobbying campaign materials, presentation at a mock school-board meeting, and class vote and discussion. First, students will participate in a class discussion about the lobbying campaigns waged by public interest groups. Then student groups will hold a planning session to discuss how to carry out their own lobbying campaign. Next, the groups each will conduct research and interview concerned citizens to provide support for their campaigns. Groups will then meet to prepare their lobbying-campaign materials. Each group will present its lobbying campaign at a mock school-board meeting. Finally, the class as a whole will vote on the most effective lobbying campaign and discuss what factors influenced its success.

OBJECTIVES

After completing this activity, students will be able to:
- define the terms *interest group* and *lobbying;*
- identify the purpose and functions of interest groups and lobbying campaigns;
- conduct a lobbying campaign;
- analyze what makes a lobbying campaign successful;
- write a persuasive letter;
- win endorsements for a cause;
- create a persuasive advertising campaign;
- give a persuasive speech;
- evaluate whether interest groups promote the public good.

LEARNING CONNECTIONS

- Learning Styles: interpersonal, linguistic, visual-spatial

- Skills Mastery: acquiring information, defining/clarifying problems, determining the strength of an argument, drawing conclusions; judging information, making comparisons, navigating the Internet, recognizing point of view, solving problems, synthesizing information, writing mastery: persuading
- *Connecting with Past Learning:* Chapter 17, Section 2—discussion of how interest groups work; Chapter 17, Section 3—discussion of interest groups and the public good

PLANNING

Purpose: You may use this activity in combination with teacher-directed lessons for this chapter, as a performance-based assessment of content mastery, or as an enrichment project.

Suggested Time: Plan to spend about five to seven 45-minute class periods on this project. Allow one class period to hold a class discussion of interest groups, introduce the activity, and organize students into groups. Give the groups one class period to plan their lobbying campaign. Allow one or two class periods for students to conduct research and find endorsements to support their campaign. Then give the groups one or two class periods to prepare their lobbying campaign materials. Finally, allow one class period for the groups to present their lobbying campaigns and hold a class vote and discussion of the campaigns.

Scale of Project: You will need enough room for students to work in groups and for the groups to present their campaigns at a mock school-board meeting. A large desk and a podium can be used to make the room look like a school-board meeting room. However, if you have a particularly large class, you may wish to reserve space in a larger area of the school such as a cafeteria or auditorium.

Group Size: Organize the class into four groups. Each group will organize and present a lobbying campaign in support of a different proposal.

Materials: Students will need posters, markers, and various other art supplies to prepare their lobbying campaign posters and advertisements. If your class has access to a video camera, a television set, and a videocassette recorder (VCR), students also may wish to prepare and present television advertisements as part of their lobbying campaigns.

Resources: Have students use their textbooks, the Internet, the library, and any other materials that you provide to complete their research. Students might also interview teachers, coaches, other students, parents, and community leaders for endorsements. Encourage students to explore and tap all available sources of information.

Preparation: Before starting the project, make copies of the Planning Guidelines and Project Task Sheet; you will need at least one copy for each group. You may also wish to make copies of the Standards for Evaluation form—which is a project-specific rubric—for students to use in preparing their lobbying campaigns.

IMPLEMENTATION

1. Give students an overview of the activity by describing its six stages. Tell students that they will first participate in a class discussion about interest groups and lobbying campaigns. They will then work in groups to create a plan for a lobbying campaign. Next, the student groups each will gather evidence and seek endorsements in support of their lobbying effort. Then the groups will prepare advertisements, posters, letters, and speeches. Finally, each group will present its lobbying campaign at a mock school-board meeting, which will be followed by a class vote and discussion of the most effective lobbying campaign.

2. To begin the class discussion of interest groups and lobbying campaigns, ask students to review the Section 2 Summary found at the end of Chapter 17. Have students identify the ways that interest groups make their concerns known to officials and to the public. *(Answers may include endorsing and giving contributions to politicians, lobbying, filing lawsuits, and influencing public opinion through mailings and newspaper and radio advertisements.)* Write the students' responses on the chalkboard. Then circle the term *lobbying* on the chalkboard and ask students to give their impres-

sions concerning whether or not lobbying promotes the public good and, if so, how.

3. Ensure that students understand the following terms: interest group, lobbying, and grassroots lobbying. If necessary, have students use the Glossary at the back of the textbook or a dictionary to write the definitions of these terms.

4. Introduce the activity by explaining that student groups will prepare mock lobbying campaigns on an issue affecting a high school. Distribute copies of the Planning Guidelines and Project Task Sheet to each group and, if you wish, copies of the Standards for Evaluation form. Organize the class into four groups. Make sure that the four interest groups are of about equal size. Assign or have each group choose one of the four interest groups shown on the Project Task Sheet. Go over the instructions to make sure that students understand the assignment.

5. Next, have the student groups each meet to brainstorm and plan a strategy for their lobbying campaign. Tell students to feel free to use a wide variety of lobbying campaign materials, including but not limited to letters, speeches, slogans and banners, mock television commercials, newspaper advertisements, protest signs, informational brochures, e-mail, a World Wide Web site, and endorsements.

6. Once students have planned their lobbying campaign, have the groups begin their research. Encourage students to find evidence of how their assigned extracurricular activity has positively affected school grades, dropout rates, or future academic or career success in other schools. Guide students in identifying people who might provide additional information or endorse their lobbying campaign. Students might also wish to research alternative methods of funding their assigned extracurricular activity.

7. After the groups have completed their research, have students prepare the materials for their lobbying campaign. Each student in the group should be responsible for at least one part of the lobbying campaign. Emphasize to the groups that their intended audience is adult school-board members.

8. Next, set up the classroom (or your reserved area of the school) to resemble a school-board meeting. If possible, have school administra-

tors, teachers, or parents play the roles of school-board members. If this is not possible, you might have students alternate as school-board members. You should play the role of the school-board president. As school-board president, you will open the meeting. Give each group 10 minutes to present its lobbying campaign. Have each student give a brief speech and present the lobbying-campaign material he or she has prepared. Finally, have the school-board members vote on which lobbying campaign was the most persuasive, and ask them to explain why. Follow up the vote with a class discussion about whether or not the lobbying campaigns represented the best interests of every student in the school.

ASSESSMENT

1. Use the Standards for Evaluation form to help you evaluate student participation in the lobbying campaign.

2. Individual grades can be based on the student's participation in creating the lobbying campaign materials.

3. An option for additional individual assessment is to have students write a short article from the perspective of a journalist covering the mock school-board meeting.

4. Alternatively, you can assess student performance by using any or all of the following rubrics from the *Alternative Assessment Handbook* on the *One-Stop Planner CD-ROM:* Rubric 1: Acquiring Information, Rubric 2: Advertisements, Rubric 3: Artwork, Rubric 9: Comparing and Contrasting, Rubric 11: Discussions, Rubric 12: Drawing Conclusions, Rubric 14: Group Activity, Rubric 16: Judging Information, Rubric 28: Posters, Rubric 29: Presentations, Rubric 30: Research, Rubric 34: Slogans and Banners, Rubric 43: Writing to Persuade.

PLANNING GUIDELINES

Your school is in serious financial trouble. The school's budget cannot afford lab equipment and textbooks, urgent repairs, teacher salaries, and many other necessary items. The members of the school board are faced with a dilemma. They must cut school programs without jeopardizing the school's well-earned reputation as an academic powerhouse. They are considering a drastic proposal: cutting all funding to sports teams, the school band, drama and art activities, and the after-school computer laboratory.

You and other concerned students want to do something to stop this proposal from affecting your school. As a member of an interest group, you will organize a lobbying campaign to convince the school board to keep extracurricular activities a vital part of your school experience.

PROJECT TASK SHEET

The High-Tech Interest Group: Prepare a lobbying campaign in support of the after-school computer laboratory. Find evidence from other schools and educational-research reports to support your argument that the computer lab enriches academic life at your school. You might also interview teachers and other experts to get their endorsement of your campaign. Each team member will be responsible for preparing a speech, letter, poster, advertisement, commercial, or other lobbying-campaign material to present to the school board.

The Sports Interest Group: Prepare a lobbying campaign in support of your school's sports programs. Find evidence from other schools and educational-research reports to support your argument that sports enrich academic life at your school. You might also interview teachers and other experts to get their endorsement of your campaign. Each team member will be responsible for preparing a speech, letter, poster, advertisement, commercial, or other lobbying-campaign material to present to the school board.

The Band Interest Group: Prepare a lobbying campaign in support of your school's band program. Find evidence from other schools and educational-research reports to support your argument that student participation in the band enriches academic life at your school. You might also interview teachers and other experts to get their endorsement of your campaign. Each team member will be responsible for preparing a speech, letter, poster, advertisement, commercial, or other lobbying-campaign material to present to the school board.

The Art and Drama Interest Group: Prepare a lobbying campaign in support of your school's art and drama programs. Find evidence from other schools and educational-research reports to support your argument that theater and the arts enrich academic life at your school. You might also interview teachers and other experts to get their endorsement of your campaign. Each team member will be responsible for preparing a speech, letter, poster, advertisement, commercial, or other lobbying-campaign material to present to the school board.

STANDARDS FOR EVALUATION

EXCELLENT

- The group's lobbying-campaign materials present well-reasoned, persuasive arguments.
- The group's presentation is creative and well organized and thoroughly explores the advantages of the group's assigned extracurricular activity.
- All group members participate fully in the lobbying campaign.

GOOD

- The group's lobbying-campaign materials present persuasive arguments.
- The group's presentation is well organized and adequately explores the advantages of the group's assigned extracurricular activity.
- All group members participate in the lobbying campaign.

ACCEPTABLE

- Most of the group's lobbying-campaign materials present persuasive arguments.
- The group's presentation is organized and explores many advantages of the group's assigned extracurricular activity.
- Most group members participate fully in the lobbying campaign.

UNACCEPTABLE

- The group's lobbying-campaign materials fail to show well-reasoned, persuasive arguments.
- The group's presentation fails to present the advantages of the group's assigned extracurricular activity.
- Few group members participate fully in the lobbying campaign.

WHAT WE STAND FOR: STATE PARTY STRATEGY SESSIONS

GOAL

In this activity students will learn about the main functions of state political parties by holding strategy sessions and a voter-registration drive aimed at winning young voters.

OVERVIEW

This project has six components: class discussion, research, group strategy sessions, preparation of materials, voter-registration drive, and vote tally and class discussion. First, students will participate in a class discussion about the role of state political parties. Then student groups will research the functions of their state's political parties. Next, the student groups will hold strategy sessions to map out how to attract young voters. Each group will then prepare materials for a voter-registration drive. Each group will set up an information booth to present its materials to fellow students and "register" voters. Finally, the class will meet to tally the number of voters and discuss the effectiveness of each strategy.

OBJECTIVES

After completing this activity, students will be able to:
- identify the roles played by state political parties;
- research a political party's platform;
- explain how a state political party influences the party platform;
- describe how a state political party organizes voter-registration drives;
- devise strategies to motivate young people to vote;
- prepare a voter-registration campaign;
- participate in political party activities;
- explain the relationship between political parties and the public good.

LEARNING CONNECTIONS

- Learning Styles: interpersonal, linguistic, visual-spatial, body-kinesthetic

- Skills Mastery: acquiring information, defining problems, drawing conclusions, judging information, navigating the Internet, recognizing point of view, solving problems, synthesizing information, writing mastery: informing, writing mastery: persuading
- *Connecting with Past Learning:* Chapter 1, Section 3—discussion of the foundations of democracy; Chapter 3, Section 1—discussion of popular sovereignty; Chapter 3, Section 3—discussion of political parties; Chapter 16, Section 3—Case Study feature, "'Rock the Vote' and 'Choose or Lose'"; Chapter 18, Section 1—discussion of the functions of political parties; Chapter 18, Section 3—discussion of political party organization; Chapter 18, Section 4—Citizenship in Action feature, "Young Politicians"

PLANNING

Purpose: You may use this activity in combination with teacher-directed lessons for this chapter, as a performance-based assessment of content mastery, or as an enrichment project.

Suggested Time: Plan to spend about five to seven 45-minute class periods on this project. Allow one class period to hold a class discussion about the role of political parties, introduce the activity, and organize groups. Give students one or two class periods to research the functions of their state's political parties. Allow one class period for student groups to hold strategy sessions. Give the groups one or two class periods to prepare their materials for the voter-registration drive. Use a lunch period or study hall for students to set up information booths to present their materials to fellow students and to "register" voters. Allow one class period to tally the number of registered voters and discuss the effectiveness of each voter-registration strategy.

Scale of Project: You will need enough room for students to work in groups and for groups to set up information booths. You may wish to reserve space for the information booths in a high-traffic area of the school, such as the cafeteria or an auditorium.

Group Size: Organize the class into at least two groups. One group will represent the Young Republicans and the other group will represent the Young Democrats. If you wish, you may identify independent parties for students to represent. Groups will break into two smaller groups.

Materials: Students will need poster boards, butcher paper, markers, and other art supplies to prepare posters, party-platform brochures, and any additional materials they choose. If students have access to high-tech tools, they may wish to prepare television commercials, sound recordings, or a World Wide Web site.

Resources: Have students use their textbooks, the Internet, the library, and any other materials that you provide to complete their research. Suggest that students use the Internet to get more information about MTV's voter registration drives and the activities of Young Republican and Young Democrat groups. If feasible, students might also wish to contact political science professors at colleges or universities in your community to learn more about state political parties and voter behavior. Encourage students to explore and tap all available sources of information.

Preparation: Before starting the project, make copies of the Planning Guidelines and Project Task Sheet; you will need at least one copy for each group. You may also wish to make copies of the Standards for Evaluation form—which is a project-specific rubric—for students to use in preparing their political strategy sessions and voter-registration drives.

IMPLEMENTATION

1. Give students an overview of the activity by describing its six stages. Tell students that they will first participate in a class discussion about the role of political parties. Then student groups will research the functions of their state's political parties. Next, the groups will hold strategy sessions to modify the party platform and voter-registration materials to attract young voters. Each group will then prepare materials for a mock voter-registration drive. The groups will set up information booths in school to "register" voters. Finally, the class will count the voters registered and hold a class discussion about the effectiveness of the voter-registration drives.

2. To begin the class discussion of political parties, review with students Section 1 of Chapter 18, entitled "Functions of Political Parties." Ask students to identify the main functions of the major political parties. *(The main functions include assisting the electoral process, helping to run government, and nominating candidates.)* Write these functions on the chalkboard, leaving enough room for students to identify specific roles under each heading. Emphasize the parties' roles in the voting process *(encourage voter registration and voting, fund-raising, distribute party literature).* Ask students whether they have a generally negative or positive opinion of how political parties participate in elections. Encourage them to explain their answers.

3. Ensure that students understand the following terms: electorate, political party, party platform, voter-registration drive, and independent party (if applicable). If necessary, have students use the Glossary at the back of the textbook or a dictionary to write the definitions of these terms.

4. Organize the class into groups. Each group will represent the youth branch of a political party. The class can be organized into two groups, with half of the class representing the Young Democrats and the other half the Young Republicans. If you wish to form additional groups, also organize the class into groups that represent independent parties identified by you or the students as important. Distribute copies of the Planning Guidelines (at least one per group) and the Project Task Sheet (at least two per group) and, if you wish, copies of the Standards for Evaluation form. Go over the instructions to make sure that students understand the assignment.

5. Have student groups meet to divide up the assignment. Each group should break down into two smaller groups. The smaller groups each will be responsible for researching one of the following state-party activities: deciding the party's platform and organizing a voter-registration drive. Then have the smaller groups begin their research. Students might contact the local office or state headquarters of their assigned political party. Each student should investigate one source of information and write a short paper summarizing his or her research.

6. Once students have completed their research, have the larger groups meet to hold strategy sessions. The smaller groups should present their research at this time. Then each group should use this information to come up with strategies that will attract young people to register to vote.

7. Have the groups prepare their materials for a voter-registration drive. Also have each group design a "ballot" box to hold the registration sheet of each voter "registered." You might wish to have an "independent observer" from a competing group make sure that no ballot-stuffing occurs. If possible, hold the voter-registration drive in a high-traffic area such as the school cafeteria so that student groups can be sure to attract the most voters.

8. After the voter-registration drive, tally the number of voters each group registered. Hold a class discussion to evaluate each party's voter-registration strategies. Have students consider what factors were most important in attracting young voters.

ASSESSMENT

1. Use the Standards for Evaluation form to help you evaluate student participation in the strategy sessions and voter-registration drives.

2. Individual grades can be based on the student's participation in creating party materials.

3. An option for additional individual assessment is to have students write a short paper summarizing their research.

4. Alternatively, you can assess student performance by using any or all of the following rubrics from the *Alternative Assessment Handbook* on the *One-Stop Planner CD-ROM:* Rubric 1: Acquiring Information, Rubric 2: Advertisements, Rubric 3: Artwork, Rubric 11: Discussions, Rubric 12: Drawing Conclusions, Rubric 14: Group Activity, Rubric 16: Judging Information, Rubric 26: Poems and Songs, Rubric 28: Posters, Rubric 30: Research, Rubric 34: Slogans and Banners, Rubric 35: Solving Problems, Rubric 43: Writing to Persuade.

PLANNING GUIDELINES

The leaders of the main political parties in your state worry that few young people are registering to vote in an upcoming election. Both parties want to attract voters aged 18 to 21. To do so, they have decided to revise their party platform to include issues that will appeal to young voters. They also want to launch a voter-registration drive and create promotional materials that will appeal to young voters.

Your school's Young Republicans and Young Democrats have been asked to help come up with a winning strategy to motivate young people to register and vote. To do so, you must first research how the state political parties take part in the electoral process. Find out how your state parties arrive at a party platform, prepare campaign and promotional materials, and organize voter-registration drives. Use this information to formulate a youth platform and prepare party materials targeted at young voters.

PROJECT TASK SHEET

Young _____

Party Platform Committee: Your committee is responsible for researching how your state political party prepares a party platform on important issues. Use this information to formulate a strategy for modifying the party platform to appeal to young voters. Keep in mind that the new platform must be faithful to the ideals of your political party. Create posters, brochures, songs, slogans and banners, television commercials, or other materials to publicize the youth-oriented changes in the party platform.

Young _____

Voter Registration Committee: Your committee is responsible for researching how your state political party organizes voter-registration drives. Use this information to formulate a strategy for holding a voter-registration drive that will appeal to young voters. Create posters, brochures, songs, slogans and banners, television commercials, or other materials to publicize your youth-oriented voter-registration drive.

STANDARDS FOR EVALUATION

EXCELLENT

- The group's party platform and voter-registration drive show a full understanding of the main functions of its assigned state political party.
- The student's strategy sessions and materials show a thorough and careful analysis of the issues that concern young voters and the promotional materials that appeal to them.
- All group members participate fully in the strategy sessions and voter-registration drive.

ACCEPTABLE

- The group's party platform and voter-registration drive show a basic understanding of the main functions of its assigned state political party.
- The student's strategy sessions and materials show a basic understanding of the issues that concern young voters and the promotional materials that appeal to them.
- Most group members participate in the strategy sessions and voter-registration drive.

GOOD

- The group's party platform and voter-registration drive show a good understanding of the main functions of its assigned state political party.
- The student's strategy sessions and promotional materials show a solid analysis of the issues that concern young voters and the promotional materials that appeal to them.
- All group members participate in the strategy sessions and voter-registration drive.

UNACCEPTABLE

- The group's party platform and voter-registration drive show a poor understanding of the main functions of its assigned state political party.
- The student's strategy sessions and materials show a poor analysis of the issues that concern young voters and the promotional materials that appeal to them.
- Few group members participate in the strategy sessions and voter-registration drive.

INSPIRE THE VOTERS: WRITE A CAMPAIGN SPEECH

GOAL

In this activity students will learn about the electoral process by writing and presenting campaign speeches for historical presidential candidates.

OVERVIEW

This project has five components: class discussion, research, speech writing, presentation of speeches, and class discussion. First, students will participate in a class discussion about the ways in which presidential campaigns have changed over the years. Then the student groups each will research the important events, issues, candidates, and election result concerning a past presidential election. Next, each student will write a short campaign speech for his or her assigned presidential candidate. Each student will then give a two- to three-minute speech to the class without revealing his or her assigned candidate's name or time period. After all the speeches have been presented, the students will try to determine the candidates' identities and discuss the differences among the various "presidential" speeches.

OBJECTIVES

After completing this activity, students will be able to:

- describe how political campaigning has changed over the years;
- identify important issues and events from past presidential campaigns;
- compare and contrast historical candidates' campaign platforms;
- discuss the relationship between political campaigns and the public good;
- write a campaign speech;
- deliver a campaign speech.

LEARNING CONNECTIONS

- Learning Styles: interpersonal, intrapersonal, linguistic
- Skills Mastery: acquiring information, defining problems, determining the strength of an argument, drawing conclusions, judging information, making comparisons, navigating the Internet, recognizing point of view, synthesizing information, writing mastery: informing, writing mastery: persuading
- *Connecting with Past Learning:* Chapter 7, Section 1—discussion of the roles of the president; Chapter 7, Section 2—discussion of early presidents and the modern presidency and Linking Government and History feature, "The President and the Media"; Chapter 19, Section 2—discussion of political campaigns and campaign financing

PLANNING

Purpose: You may use this activity in combination with teacher-directed lessons for this chapter, as a performance-based assessment of content mastery, or as an enrichment project.

Suggested Time: Plan to spend about five to seven 45-minute class periods on this project. Allow one class period to hold a group discussion about political campaigns, introduce the activity, and organize groups. Allow two or three class periods for the student groups to research the important issues, events, candidates, and outcome of a past presidential election. Have students write and practice their speeches at home. Allow two class periods for students to present their speeches to the class. You might need an additional class period for students to determine the candidates' identities and discuss the differences in the presidential speeches from the various historical periods.

Scale of Project: You will need enough room for students to work in small groups and for students to present their speeches in front of the class.

Group Size: Organize the class into two groups of four students each. Organize the rest of the class into pairs of students. Each two- or four-person group will research a particular presidential election. Individual students will then write and present campaign speeches for their assigned presidential candidates.

Materials: Students may use various art supplies to prepare a poster representing the main slogans and ideas of their assigned presidential candidate's campaign. If you have access to a video camera, television, and videocassette recorder (VCR), you may wish to videotape the speeches for later playback and review.

Resources: Have students use their textbooks, the Internet, the library, and any other materials that you provide to complete their research. If feasible, students may wish to contact political science or government professors at colleges or universities in your community to learn more about their assigned presidential candidates. Encourage students to explore and tap all available sources of information.

Preparation: Before starting the project, make copies of the Planning Guidelines and Project Task Sheet; you will need at least one copy for each two- and four-person group. You may also wish to make copies of the Standards for Evaluation form—which is a project-specific rubric—for students to use in preparing their presidential campaign speeches.

IMPLEMENTATION

1. Give students an overview of the activity by describing its five stages. First, students will participate in a class discussion about how presidential campaigns have changed over the years. Then student groups will research the events, important issues, main candidates, and outcome of a past presidential election. Next, each student will write a short campaign speech for his or her assigned presidential candidate. Each student will then present a two- to three-minute campaign speech to the class without revealing his or her assigned candidate's name or time period. After all the speeches have been presented to the class, the students will try to guess the candidates' identities and discuss what makes campaign speeches effective. Students may also "vote" in each of the elections to assess the speeches.

2. To begin the class discussion of presidential campaigns, ask students to review the Section 2 Summary found at the end of Chapter 19. Have students identify the ways that presidential campaigns have changed since the 1700s. *(Candidates have become more visible; the media has become more involved; polling has become more important.)* Write the students' responses on the chalkboard. Then ask students to evaluate what aspects of a candidate's campaign are the most important. They might consider speeches, participation in debates, fund-raising, and television advertisements.

3. Organize two groups of four students. The rest of the class will be organized into groups of two students each. Distribute copies of the Planning Guidelines and Project Task Sheet to each group and, if you wish, copies of the Standards for Evaluation form. Assign or have groups choose an election year from the list on the Planning Guidelines. The two groups of four students should choose between the election of 1860 and the election of 1912. Go over the instructions to make sure that students understand the assignment. Emphasize that students should not tell other groups what election year or candidates they are researching.

4. Have student groups begin their research. Point out that they should investigate the major issues, events, candidates, and outcome of their assigned election year. Instruct each student to choose a presidential candidate to research. Students should learn about the candidate's personality, ideals, and political beliefs. They should also try to determine their candidate's campaign strategy. Have each student write a brief summary of the research.

5. Once students have completed their research, have students write a short campaign speech for their candidate. Tell students to limit their speeches to no more than three minutes so that all candidates have enough time to speak in two class periods. If you have a smaller class or more time, you might consider allowing students to give longer speeches. Advise students that their campaign speeches should persuasively argue why their candidate is the best person to lead the nation at that particular time in history. They should keep in mind the issues and events that are most important to voters in that year. Remind students that they should not reveal to anyone their candidate's name or election year.

6. After students have written and practiced their speeches, have them present their speeches in front of the class. You can introduce each election year by giving a short teaser, or hint, to set the scene. Explain that the students listening to

the speech should try to guess the identity and election year of each candidate. They can use the "Name That Candidate" form to write down their guesses. Encourage students to take notes about the things they liked about each speech. If you have access to a video camera, you might wish to videotape the speeches for later playback and review.

7. Once all the speeches have been delivered, have students turn in their "Name That Candidate" forms. Tally the number of votes for each candidate and write the results on the chalkboard. Hand back the forms and have students reveal the identities of their candidates. Then have students discuss the campaign speeches and determine which ones were the most persuasive, informative, or memorable.

ASSESSMENT

1. Use the Standards for Evaluation form to help you evaluate student participation in the campaign-speech activity.

2. Individual grades can be based on student speeches.

3. An option for additional individual assessment is to have students write a short summary of the issues, events, candidates, and outcome of their assigned election campaign.

4. Alternatively, you can assess student performance by using any or all of the following rubrics from the *Alternative Assessment Handbook* on the *One-Stop Planner CD-ROM:* Rubric 1: Acquiring Information, Rubric 11: Discussions, Rubric 12: Drawing Conclusions, Rubric 14: Group Activity, Rubric 16: Judging Information, Rubric 18: Listening, Rubric 24: Oral Presentations, Rubric 28: Posters, Rubric 30: Research, Rubric 42: Writing to Inform, Rubric 43: Writing to Persuade.

PLANNING GUIDELINES

Imagine working as a speechwriter for a past presidential candidate. You would have to get to know your candidate's personality, ideals, and vision. You would also have to find out what issues and events most concerned voters in the year that your candidate ran for president. Finally, you would have to be creative in coming up with a persuasive, exciting speech that fit your candidate and appealed to the voters.

Research, write, and present a speech for one of the presidential candidates listed below. But do not give away your candidate's name or the year of the campaign in your speech. The rest of the class will guess the identity of your presidential candidate by the clues that you give about your candidate's views and the important events and issues of that campaign year.

1796	John Adams		Theodore Roosevelt
	Thomas Jefferson		William Howard Taft
1828	Andrew Jackson		Eugene Debs
	John Quincy Adams	1924	Calvin Coolidge
1860	Abraham Lincoln		John W. Davis
	Stephen Douglas	1932	Franklin D. Roosevelt
	John Breckinridge		Herbert Hoover
	John Bell	1948	Harry S. Truman
1868	Ulysses S. Grant		Thomas E. Dewey
	Horatio Seymour	1960	John F. Kennedy
1896	William McKinley		Richard M. Nixon
	William Jennings Bryan	1980	Ronald W. Reagan
1908	William Howard Taft		Jimmy Carter
	William Jennings Bryan	1992	William J. Clinton
1912	Woodrow Wilson		George Bush

PROJECT TASK SHEET

Name That Candidate

Use the headings below to mark your guesses of the presidential candidates' identities. As each student gives a speech, try to guess the identity of the candidate. Also, cast your vote for a candidate from each presidential campaign. Explain the reasons for your vote.

Student's Name	Candidate	Election Year	Vote	Explain Your Vote

PLANNING GUIDELINES

EXCELLENT

- The student's research summary shows a thorough understanding of the issues, events, candidates, and outcome of his or her assigned election year.
- The student's speech persuasively presents the candidate's personality and political ideals.
- Group members participate fully in the research and speeches.

GOOD

- The student's research summary shows a good understanding of the issues, events, candidates, and outcome of his or her assigned election year.
- The student's speech presents the candidate's personality and political ideals.
- Group members participate in the research and speeches.

ACCEPTABLE

- The student's research summary shows some understanding of the issues, events, candidates, and outcome of his or her assigned election year.
- The student's speech summarizes the candidate's political ideals.
- Most group members participate fully in the research and speeches.

UNACCEPTABLE

- The student's research summary fails to show an understanding of the issues, events, candidates, and outcome of his or her assigned election year.
- The student fails to summarize the candidate's political ideals.
- Few group members participate fully in the research and speeches.

DEBATING STATE TERM LIMITS

GOAL

In this activity students will learn about an issue affecting state government by holding a debate on state term limits.

OVERVIEW

This project has four components: class discussion, research, debate on an issue, and class discussion. First, students will participate in a class discussion about state government. Then student groups will research arguments for and against setting term limits for state politicians. The class will then hold a debate on term limits. Finally, the class as a whole will evaluate the debate and vote on the issue of state term limits.

OBJECTIVES

After completing this activity, students will be able to:

- identify the three branches of state government;
- explain the roles of the three branches of state government;
- explain how citizens can influence state government;
- identify arguments in favor of state term limits;
- identify arguments against state term limits;
- assess the purpose and effectiveness of term limits;
- prepare pro and con arguments for a debate;
- participate in a debate;
- state a point of view concerning the issue of state term limits.

LEARNING CONNECTIONS

- Learning Styles: interpersonal, linguistic
- Skills Mastery: acquiring information, defining/clarifying problems, determining the strength of an argument, drawing conclusions, judging information, recognizing point of view, synthesizing information, writing mastery: informing
- *Connecting with Past Learning:* Chapter 6, Section 1—discussion of congressional term limits; Chapter 20, Section 1—discussion of

the states; Chapter 20, Section 2—discussion of the organization of state government

PLANNING

Purpose: You may use this activity in combination with teacher-directed lessons for this chapter, as a performance-based assessment of content mastery, or as an enrichment project.

Suggested Time: Plan to spend about five to six 45-minute class periods on this project. Allow one class period to hold a class discussion of state government, introduce the activity, and organize students into groups. Allow two or three class periods for students to research the issue of term limits. Then allow one class period for groups to debate term limits. You will need an additional class period to discuss the outcome of the debate and hold a class vote on the issue of term limits.

Scale of Project: You will need enough room for students to work in groups and to hold a debate. However, if you have a particularly large class or more than one debate going on, you may wish to reserve a larger area in the school such as the cafeteria or auditorium.

Group Size: Organize the class into two groups. One group will prepare arguments for and debate state term limits; the other will oppose and debate state term limits. If you wish to have students work in smaller groups, organize students into four groups and have each pair of groups conduct a separate state term-limits debate.

Materials: For ease of reference during the debate, students might use index cards to briefly summarize their evidence and arguments.

Resources: Have students use their textbooks, the Internet, the library, and any other materials that you provide to complete their research. If feasible, students may wish to contact government or political science professors at colleges or universities in your community to learn more about the issue of state term limits. Encourage students to explore and tap all available sources of information.

Preparation: Before starting the project, make copies of the Planning Guidelines and Project Task Sheet; you will need at least one copy for each group. You may also wish to make copies of the Standards for Evaluation form—which is a project-specific rubric—for students to use in preparing their debate materials.

IMPLEMENTATION

1. Give students an overview of the activity by describing its four stages. Tell students that they will first participate in a class discussion about how state governments are organized. They will then work in groups to research the issue of term limits for state legislators. Then student groups will take part in a class debate about state term limits. Finally, the class as a whole will decide who "won" the debate and vote on the issue of state term limits.

2. To begin the class discussion of state government, ask students to review the Section 1 and Section 2 summaries found at the end of Chapter 20. Have students identify the three branches of state government. *(The three branches are the executive branch, the legislative branch, and the judicial branch.)* Write students' responses on the chalkboard and have students identify the main functions of each branch. *(executive branch: carry out laws; legislative branch: make laws; judicial branch: try accused criminals and decide constitutionality of laws)* Then have students identify the formal mechanisms that citizens can use to influence state government. *(initiative, referendum, recall)* Have students provide examples of citizens working to reform state government by an initiative, referendum, or recall. Review with students the discussion of congressional term limits found in Chapter 6, and explain that citizens have sought more control over state legislatures by implementing term limits for state politicians.

3. Ensure that students understand the following terms: initiative, referendum, recall, term limits, and rebuttal. If necessary, have students use the Glossary at the back of the textbook or a dictionary to write the definitions of these terms.

4. Organize the class into two (or four) groups. Assign one group to research and prepare arguments in favor of state term limits, and the other group to research and prepare arguments opposing state term limits. Distribute copies of the Planning Guidelines and Project Task Sheet to each group and, if you wish, copies of the Standards for Evaluation form. Go over the instructions on the Planning Guidelines to make sure that students understand the assignment. Point out to students that they should not be limited to finding evidence only for the arguments listed in the Project Task Sheet. They should also include any additional arguments that they find in the course of their research. Also, students should find evidence for rebuttals against the opposing group's arguments.

5. Have student groups meet to assign research tasks. To conduct the research, the larger groups might break down into smaller groups or pairs of students. Each smaller group might be responsible for finding evidence for one of the arguments listed on the Project Task Sheet. To help students begin their research, you might direct students to find out whether their state has sought to institute term limits for state politicians. Consider assigning each student to write a two-page report that summarizes how their state (or another state, if their state does not have term limits) instituted term limits and the impact term limits have had on state government. This activity should help students identify arguments for and against state term limits. Suggest that students summarize their evidence and arguments on index cards for use during the debate.

6. Once students have completed their research, have the class hold a debate on state term limits. Set up chairs, tables, or desks in the classroom or other designated area so that the opposing groups face each other. You might either have the entire class debate the issue or pair up smaller groups from opposing sides to debate the issue. For the class debate, you may wish to act as moderator of the debate. For the smaller group debates, have a student volunteer act as moderator. The moderator should describe the issue and then identify the position of each group. Have the groups take turns presenting their arguments. Allow each side three minutes to present each argument, and give the opposing side two minutes to offer a rebuttal of each argument. Remind students that they should make their arguments as persuasive as possible. You might consider having

another teacher, lawyer, or government official observe the debates and decide which side "won" the debate.

7. Finally, hold a class discussion about the debate. Ask students to evaluate which arguments were the most persuasive. Encourage them to explain whether the debate changed their opinion about the issue of term limits. Conclude the discussion by asking whether students think that term limits make state government more accountable to the voters. Then hold a secret ballot to determine whether the majority of the class supports or opposes term limits for state politicians.

ASSESSMENT

1. Use the Standards for Evaluation form to help you evaluate student participation in the term-limit debate.

2. Individual grades can be based on the student's participation in the debate.

3. An option for additional individual assessment is to have students write a short report on a state campaign for term limits.

4. Alternatively, you can assess student performance by using any or all of the following rubrics from the *Alternative Assessment Handbook* on the *One-Stop Planner CD-ROM:* Rubric 1: Acquiring Information, Rubric 10: Debates, Rubric 11: Discussions, Rubric 12: Drawing Conclusions, Rubric 14: Group Activity, Rubric 16: Judging Information, Rubric 18: Listening, Rubric 30: Research, Rubric 42: Writing to Inform.

PLANNING GUIDELINES

A group of citizens in your state has prepared a new initiative for an upcoming election. If voters approve it, the initiative would make it illegal for elected state politicians to serve more than two terms. Hold a debate to evaluate the merits of this initiative.

PROJECT TASK SHEET

Arguments in Favor of Term Limits

Argument 1: Term limits keep lobbyists from exerting too much influence on legislators.

Evidence: _____

Evidence: _____

Argument 2: Term limits eliminate corrupt or inefficient politicians.

Evidence: _____

Evidence: _____

Argument 3: Term limits make politicians more responsive to voters.

Evidence: _____

Evidence: _____

Argument 4: The majority of citizens support term limits.

Evidence: _____

Evidence: _____

Arguments Against Term Limits

Argument 1: Term limits are unconstitutional.

Evidence: _____

Evidence: _____

Argument 2: Term limits limit voters' choices.

Evidence: _____

Evidence: _____

Argument 3: Term limits keep talented, experienced lawmakers out of office.

Evidence: _____

Evidence: _____

Argument 4: Term limits create an unstable, inexperienced legislature.

Evidence: _____

Evidence: _____

STANDARDS FOR EVALUATION

EXCELLENT

- The group's evidence for or against term limits shows a thorough understanding of how term limits affect state government.
- The group presents organized, persuasive, and clear arguments for or against term limits.
- All group members participate fully in the debate on term limits.

GOOD

- The group's evidence for or against term limits shows a complete understanding of how term limits affect state government.
- The group presents persuasive, clear arguments for or against term limits.
- All group members participate in the debate on term limits.

ACCEPTABLE

- The group's evidence for or against term limits shows an understanding of how term limits affect state government.
- The group presents persuasive arguments for or against term limits.
- Most group members participate fully in the debate on term limits.

UNACCEPTABLE

- The group's evidence for or against term limits fails to show an understanding of how term limits affect state government.
- The group's arguments for or against term limits are unpersuasive.
- Few group members participate fully in the debate on term limits.

LOCAL GOVERNMENTS AND TEEN CURFEWS

GOAL

In this activity students will learn how their local government works by holding a mock local-government meeting on the issue of teen curfews.

OVERVIEW

This project has four components: class discussion, research, mock local-government meeting, and evaluations and class vote. First, students will participate in a class discussion about local government. Then student groups will research how their local government works and why teen curfews have been instituted. The class will then hold a mock local-government meeting on the issue of teen curfews. Finally, the class as a whole will evaluate the local-government meeting and vote on whether a teen curfew should be implemented in their area.

OBJECTIVES

After completing this activity, students will be able to:

- identify the main types of local governments;
- explain what type of local government their community has;
- explain how citizens can influence local government;
- identify arguments in favor of teen curfews;
- identify arguments against teen curfews;
- assess the purpose and effectiveness of teen curfews;
- prepare testimony for a local-government meeting;
- state a point of view concerning the issue of teen curfews.

LEARNING CONNECTIONS

- Learning Styles: interpersonal, intrapersonal, linguistic
- Skills Mastery: acquiring information, defining/clarifying problems, determining the strength of an argument, drawing conclusions, judging information, navigating the Internet, recognizing point of view, solving problems, synthesizing information, writing mastery: informing
- **Connecting with Past Learning:** Chapter 1, Section 1—discussion of the government's role in maintaining order; Chapter 21, Section 2—discussion of local government organization

PLANNING

Purpose: You may use this activity in combination with teacher-directed lessons for this chapter, as a performance-based assessment of content mastery, or as an enrichment project.

Suggested Time: Plan to spend about five to seven 45-minute class periods on this project. Allow one class period to hold a class discussion of local government, introduce the activity, and organize students into groups. Allow two or three class periods for students to research their local government and the issue of teen curfews. Then allow two class periods for the class to hold a mock local-government meeting on teen curfews. You may need an additional class period to allow students to discuss the local-government meeting and evaluate what impact citizens can have on local government.

Scale of Project: You will need enough room for students to work in groups and to hold a mock local-government meeting. You might set up tables at the front of the classroom for the local-government leaders and provide a podium from which students may give their testimony. If you wish to invite other teachers and classes to serve as members of the audience, reserve space in a larger area of the school such as the cafeteria or auditorium.

Group Size: Organize the class into four groups of roughly equal size. Each group will play one of the roles in the local-government meeting summarized on the Project Task Sheet.

Materials: Students might wish to use poster board and art materials to make posters with slogans for or against teen curfews. If students have access to a video camera, television, and video-cassette recorder (VCR), they might wish to film the local-government meeting for later review.

Resources: Have students use their textbooks, the Internet, the library, and any other materials that you provide to complete their research. If possible, have students attend a public meeting of their local government to see how meetings are run and decisions are made. Students might also consult local political leaders, police officers, or the World Wide Web site of their city government for more information about how governmental decisions are made. Encourage students to explore and tap all available sources of information.

Preparation: Before starting the project, make copies of the Planning Guidelines and Project Task Sheet; you will need at least one copy for each group. You may also wish to make copies of the Standards for Evaluation form—which is a project-specific rubric—for students to use in preparing their roles in the local-government meeting.

IMPLEMENTATION

1. Give students an overview of the activity by describing its four stages. Tell students that they will first participate in a class discussion about how local governments are organized. Then student groups will research how their local government works and why teen curfews have been instituted in various locales around the country. The class will then hold a mock local-government meeting on the issue of teen curfews. Finally, the class will evaluate citizen participation in the local-government meeting and vote on a teen curfew for their community.

2. To begin the class discussion of local government, ask students to review the Section 2 Summary found at the end of Chapter 21. Have students identify three types of municipal government. *(mayor-council, council-manager, commission)* Write the three types of government on the chalkboard and have students describe who makes decisions in each one. Ask students to speculate about how much influence citizens have in each type of government. Then have students identify their own city's type of government.

3. Ensure that students understand the following terms: county, township, municipality, mayor-council system, council-manager system, city manager, and commission. If necessary, have students use the Glossary at the back of the textbook or a dictionary to write the definitions of these terms.

4. Organize the class into four groups. Assign or allow each group to choose one of the roles outlined on the Project Task Sheet. Distribute copies of the Planning Guidelines and Project Task Sheet to each group and, if you wish, copies of the Standards for Evaluation form. Go over the instructions to make sure that students understand the assignment. Stress to students that their research should focus on citizen participation in local government.

5. Next, have the student groups meet to divide the research tasks. The Local-Government Group will research the three types of municipal government and explain the workings of their local government. The Police Group will be responsible for determining the organizational structure of the police department and whether it reports to the municipal government. The Police Group should also research how teen curfews have affected crime rates in other cities. The "Support Teen Curfews" Group should identify a wide range of people in support of teen curfews and explain their reasons for supporting this measure. The "End Teen Curfews" Group should do the same for people and arguments against teen curfews. Have each student write a two-page report that summarizes the research of his or her group.

6. Once students have completed their research, have the class hold a mock local-government meeting in which citizens air their views concerning the issue of teen curfews. Set up a long table for the local-government leaders at the front of the classroom or other designated area. A podium can be placed in front of the table so that students can present their testimony. The Local-Government Group should begin the meeting by explaining what form of government your city has and comparing it to other types of local governments. They then should explain how public meetings are run in your city. One of the Local-Government Group members should set the rules for how long each person is allowed to testify and explain any other rules of order that might affect the speakers. To begin the meeting, the student should explain that the public will now give

testimony about teen curfews. After all students have presented their testimony, members of the Local-Government Group can weigh the testimony and make a decision about whether or not to implement a teen curfew in their community.

7. Finally, hold a class discussion about the outcome of the local-government meeting. Ask students to evaluate which testimony was the most important in influencing the local government's decision. Then hold a secret ballot to determine whether the majority of the class supports or opposes teen curfews.

ASSESSMENT

1. Use the Standards for Evaluation form to help you evaluate student participation in the local-government meeting.

2. Individual grades can be based on the student's participation in the local-government meeting.

3. An option for additional individual assessment is to have students write a short report on their research findings.

4. Alternatively, you can assess student performance by using any or all of the following rubrics from the *Alternative Assessment Handbook* on the *One-Stop Planner CD-ROM:* Rubric 1: Acquiring Information, Rubric 11: Discussions, Rubric 12: Drawing Conclusions, Rubric 14: Group Activity, Rubric 16: Judging Information, Rubric 18: Listening, Rubric 24: Oral Presentations, Rubric 28: Posters, Rubric 30: Research, Rubric 34: Slogans and Banners, Rubric 42: Writing to Inform.

PLANNING GUIDELINES

Your local government is deciding whether or not to institute a teen curfew in your city. It is considering a plan to prohibit people under the age of 18 from being outdoors after 10 o'clock at night. Civic leaders, parents, police officers, students, and other concerned citizens all have strong opinions for or against teen curfews. Hold a mock meeting of your local government to decide whether your community should enforce a teen curfew. Each of the groups below will participate in this meeting.

PROJECT TASK SHEET

The Local-Government Group: Your group will be responsible for researching and summarizing the four main types of local government. The students in your group will also find out what form of government your town or city has and how key decisions are made. You will be responsible for presenting this information to the class at the start of the local-government meeting. Your group will represent local government leaders and run a mock meeting modeled after your own local government. You will determine how much time each speaker has to offer testimony and the order of speakers. Finally, your group should weigh all public testimony and decide whether a teen curfew should be instituted and enforced.

....

The Police Group: Your group will be responsible for researching the organization and decision-making power of your local police department. You should find out how your local police department is organized and its relationship to local government. Also find out how the police department would be involved in initiating and enforcing a teen curfew in your town or city. Your group will also research crime statistics to find out whether teen curfews in other areas have helped to reduce crime rates. During the local-government meeting, group members will play the roles of Police Chief and police officers and offer testimony in support of teen curfews. Officers should offer suggestions about how the curfew should be enforced and how violators should be punished.

....

The "Support Teen Curfews" Group: Your group will be responsible for researching arguments in favor of teen curfews. Each group member should research a different town or city that has a teen curfew and determine the benefits of this policy. During the local-government meeting, members can play the roles of a wide range of concerned citizens who support a teen curfew, including students, parents, judges, businesspeople, religious leaders, and teachers.

....

The "End Teen Curfews" Group: Your group will be responsible for researching arguments against teen curfews. Each group member should research a different town or city that has a teen curfew and determine the drawbacks of this policy. During the local-government meeting, members can play the roles of a wide range of concerned citizens who oppose a teen curfew, including students, parents, businesspeople, judges, lawyers, and teachers.

STANDARDS FOR EVALUATION

EXCELLENT

- The group's research shows a thorough understanding of how citizens offer input for an important local-government decision.
- The group members' role-playing thoroughly expresses the responsibilities or interests of their assigned roles.
- All group members participate fully in the research and local-government meeting.

GOOD

- The group's research shows a complete understanding of how citizens offer input for an important local-government decision.
- The group members' role-playing expresses the responsibilities or interests of their assigned roles.
- All group members participate in the research and local-government meeting.

ACCEPTABLE

- The group's research shows a basic understanding of how citizens offer input for an important local-government decision.
- The group members' role-playing expresses some of the responsibilities or interests of their assigned roles.
- Most group members participate fully in the research and local-government meeting.

UNACCEPTABLE

- The group's research fails to show an understanding of how citizens offer input for an important local-government decision.
- The group members' role-playing fails to express the responsibilities or interests of their assigned roles.
- Few group members participate fully in the research and local-government meeting.

A DAY IN THE LIFE OF CAPITALISM, SOCIALISM, AND COMMUNISM

GOAL

In this activity students will compare and contrast life under capitalism, socialism, and communism by creating a portrait gallery of each system.

OVERVIEW

This project has five components: class discussion, research, preparation of portraits, tour of portrait "galleries," and final class discussion. First, students will participate in a class discussion about capitalism, socialism, and communism. Then student groups will research countries that represent each of these systems. Students will then prepare portraits to display in a mock gallery show. Next, students will present their portraits at a gallery opening. Finally, students will participate in a class discussion to compare and contrast these three systems.

OBJECTIVES

After completing this activity, students will be able to:

- define the terms *capitalism, socialism,* and *communism;*
- explain how these three systems differ;
- describe what life is like under each of these systems;
- research politics and economics through pictures;
- show political and economic information in pictures;
- prepare a portrait;
- organize a portrait gallery show.

LEARNING CONNECTIONS

- Learning Styles: body-kinesthetic, interpersonal, visual-spatial
- Skills Mastery: acquiring information, judging information, making comparisons, navigating the Internet, synthesizing information, writing mastery: describing
- *Connecting with Past Learning:* Chapter 22, Section 1, Section 2, and Section 3—discussion of comparative political and economic systems

PLANNING

Purpose: You may use this activity in combination with teacher-directed lessons for this chapter, as a performance-based assessment of content mastery, or as an enrichment project.

Suggested Time: Plan to spend about six to eight 45-minute class periods on this project. Allow one class period to hold a class discussion of the three systems, introduce the activity, and organize students into groups. Allow two or three class periods for students to research various countries. Give students two or three class periods to prepare their portraits and set up their portrait galleries. Finally, allow one class period for students to present their portraits at a mock gallery opening and discuss the differences in ways of life under each type of system.

Scale of Project: You will need enough room for students to work in groups and to display their portraits. If you wish to invite other teachers and classes to the mock gallery openings, reserve space in a larger area of the school such as the cafeteria or auditorium.

Group Size: Organize the class into three groups of roughly equal size. Each group will research one of the three economic systems. In each group, individuals or pairs of students will research a particular country and prepare portraits for the gallery opening.

Materials: Students can use a wide variety of art materials such as poster board, butcher paper, paint, chalk, markers, and so on to create their portraits. Students also may wish to use brown construction paper or thin strips of wood to make "frames" for their portraits.

Resources: Have students use their textbooks, the Internet, the library, and any other materials that you provide to complete their research. If possible, show students examples from an art history book of portraits painted of the emerging capitalist classes beginning in the sixteenth century. Students also may wish to contact history, art history, or political science professors at colleges and universities in your community to learn more about the three political and economic systems. Encourage students to explore and tap all available sources of information.

Preparation: Before starting the project, make copies of the Planning Guidelines and Project Task Sheet; you will need at least one copy for each student or pair of students. You may also wish to make copies of the Standards for Evaluation form—which is a project-specific rubric—for students to use in preparing their portrait galleries.

IMPLEMENTATION

1. Give students an overview of the activity by describing its five stages. Tell students that they will first participate in a class discussion about capitalism, socialism, and communism. Then student groups will find photographic evidence that shows what life is like under these systems. Students will then design and prepare portraits that show what daily life is like under these different political and economic systems. Students will next present their portraits at a mock gallery opening. Finally, the class will hold a discussion to compare and contrast ways of life under these three systems.

2. To begin the class discussion of the three systems, ask students to review the Summary found at the end of Chapter 22. Then write the following headings on the chalkboard: *Capitalism, Socialism, Communism.* Point out that an "entrepreneur" is a type of person who is associated with the economic system of capitalism. Ask students to identify other types of people associated with each of the three systems. *(For example, capitalism: capitalist, consumer, bourgeoisie; socialism: socialist, labor union member, bureaucrat, worker, manager; communism: peasant, proletariat or worker, revolutionary, Bolshevik, Communist Party leader, collective-farm manager.)* Students may need to review the chapter to find examples of different types of people.

3. Ensure that students understand the following terms: capitalism, entrepreneur, capitalist, consumer, socialism, socialist, bourgeoisie, proletariat, communism, vanguard, Bolsheviks, and Communist Party. If necessary, have students use the Glossary at the back of the textbook or a dictionary to write the definitions of these terms.

4. Organize the class into three groups of roughly equal size. Assign or have each group choose one of the three systems under study. Distribute copies of the Planning Guidelines and Project Task Sheet to each group and, if you wish, copies of the Standards for Evaluation form. Go over the instructions to make sure that students understand the assignment. Have students meet in their groups to identify which countries have the economic or political system they have been assigned. The groups should then assign a specific country for each student or pair of students to research.

5. Have students begin their research. Stress that students will be looking for photographs, paintings, pictures, and other visual clues that document what life is like under capitalism, socialism, or communism. Tell students that they should look for illustrative materials that show people's economic, political, and social activities under a particular system. Also tell students that they should locate at least two photographs for their assigned country. Have students each write a two-page report analyzing one photograph they have found. The report should explain what the photograph reveals about life under a particular economic or political system.

6. Once students have completed their research, have students meet in groups to review the visual material they have found. Have each group member choose a particular country and type of person to represent in a portrait. Using details from the visual material they have collected, students should paint, draw, or create a collage of a person or group of people. Stress that students will not be graded on artistic merit but on the content of their portraits. The details and background of the portraits should illustrate what life is like under capitalism, socialism, or communism. Encourage groups to depict a wide range of people in different political, economic, and social situations. For example, one portrait might show an entrepreneur raising money for his company, a worker at a Communist Party meeting, or a socialist bureaucrat at home with his or her family. Have the members of each group arrange their portraits for display in a mock gallery.

7. Finally, have the members of each group hold a mock gallery opening to present their portraits. Group members should conduct a tour of their gallery for the rest of the class and any others who have been invited. Each student should explain what aspects of the political or economic system the portrait shows. After all tours have been given, the class should hold a discussion to compare and contrast life under the three systems.

ASSESSMENT

1. Use the Standards for Evaluation form to help you evaluate student participation in the portrait gallery activity.

2. Individual grades can be based on student-created portraits.

3. An option for additional individual assessment is to have students write a short report analyzing a particular photograph.

4. Alternatively, you can assess student performance by using any or all of the following rubrics from the *Alternative Assessment Handbook* on the *One-Stop Planner CD-ROM:* Rubric 1: Acquiring Information, Rubric 3: Artwork, Rubric 8: Collages, Rubric 9: Comparing and Contrasting, Rubric 11: Discussions, Rubric 14: Group Activity, Rubric 29: Presentations, Rubric 30: Research, Rubric 40: Writing to Describe.

PLANNING GUIDELINES

During the Middle Ages in Europe, most paintings were of Catholic saints. The wealthy Catholic Church helped support artists, who painted scenes from the Bible and other religious images. As capitalism began to take hold in Europe, however, the situation began to change. Newly wealthy merchants and bankers paid artists to paint their portraits.

These portraits are important not only as works of art but also as historical documents. They reveal details about what daily life was like for members of the new capitalist classes. For example, Belgian artist Quentin Metsys's painting "Money Changer and His Wife" (1514) shows a solemn banker counting money in a plain room. His wife, who sits next to him and has a sad expression on her face, is reading a prayer book. "Georg Gisze, a German Merchant in London," painted in 1532 by German artist Hans Holbein the Younger, is another revealing portrait. It shows the young merchant in his office writing a letter to his brother, with a scale, books, money, and other "tools of the trade" beside him.

What kinds of portraits would provide similar details about life in capitalist, socialist, or communist nations today? As part of an art-gallery team, your assignment is to research what life is like under one of these systems and create a portrait gallery of the people who live under each system.

PROJECT TASK SHEET

A Day in the Life of Capitalism: Your group will be responsible for researching and preparing portraits of people who live and work in capitalist nations. Each student or pair of students will research a different capitalist country. Students will find photographs, paintings, and other visual materials that show people involved in economic, political, or social activities that typify capitalism. You will then use these visual materials to paint, draw, or create collage-style portraits. The style of dress, details, and background should show a scene typical of life in a capitalist country.

....

A Day in the Life of Socialism: Your group will be responsible for researching and preparing portraits of people who live and work in socialist nations. Each student or pair of students will research a different socialist country. Students will find photographs, paintings, and other visual materials that show people involved in economic, political, or social activities that typify socialism. You will then use these visual materials to paint, draw, or create collage-style portraits. The style of dress, details, and background should show a scene typical of life in a socialist country.

....

A Day in the Life of Communism: Your group will be responsible for researching and preparing portraits of people who live and work in communist nations. Each student or pair of students will research a different communist country. Students will find photographs, paintings, and other visual materials that show people involved in economic, political, or social activities that typify communism. You will then use these visual materials to paint, draw, or create collage-style portraits. The style of dress, details, and background should show a scene typical of life in a communist country.

STANDARDS FOR EVALUATION

EXCELLENT

- The group's portraits clearly and creatively present the economic, political, and social characteristics of capitalism, socialism, or communism.
- The group's gallery shows a wide range of people who accurately represent what life is like in capitalist, socialist, or communist nations.
- All group members participate fully in the research and preparation of the portraits.

GOOD

- The group's portraits clearly present the economic, political, and social characteristics of capitalism, socialism, or communism.
- The group's gallery shows a range of people who accurately represent what life is like in capitalist, socialist, or communist nations.
- All group members participate in the research and preparation of the portraits.

ACCEPTABLE

- The group's portraits present the economic, political, and social characteristics of capitalism, socialism, or communism.
- The group's gallery shows a range of people who represent what life is like in capitalist, socialist, or communist nations.
- Most group members participate fully in the research and preparation of the portraits.

UNACCEPTABLE

- The group's portraits fail to present the economic, political, and social characteristics of capitalism, socialism, or communism.
- The group's gallery shows only a few people who represent what life is like in capitalist, socialist, or communist nations.
- Few group members participate fully in the research and preparation of the portraits.

INTERNATIONAL CRISIS: THE UN SECURITY COUNCIL AT WORK

GOAL

In this activity students will learn about the United Nations by participating in a mock UN Security Council meeting.

OVERVIEW

This project has four components: class discussion, research, Security Council meeting, and final class discussion. First, students will participate in a class discussion about the United Nations. Then students will research the stance toward nuclear proliferation of a particular country that is a member of the UN Security Council. Next, students will hold a mock Security Council meeting. Finally, the class will discuss the outcome of the Security Council meeting and determine whether the Security Council is an effective organization for solving international crises.

OBJECTIVES

After completing this activity, students will be able to:
- describe the main divisions and functions of the United Nations;
- discuss the role of the United States in the United Nations;
- identify the permanent members of the UN Security Council;
- explain how the Security Council deals with international crises;
- describe the stance of foreign nations on nuclear proliferation;
- debate an issue that has international implications;
- understand the points of view of many nations;
- weigh competing arguments;
- recognize the difficulty in reaching consensus among different nations.

LEARNING CONNECTIONS

- Learning Styles: interpersonal, linguistic
- Skills Mastery: acquiring information, defining/clarifying problems, determining the

strength of an argument, drawing conclusions, judging information, navigating the Internet, recognizing point of view, solving problems, synthesizing information, writing mastery: informing
- **Connecting with Past Learning:** Chapter 10, Section 1—discussion of United States foreign-policy goals; Chapter 10, Section 4—discussion of defense alliances; Chapter 23, Section 1—discussion of collective security

PLANNING

Purpose: You may use this activity in combination with teacher-directed lessons for this chapter, as a performance-based assessment of content mastery, or as an enrichment project.

Suggested Time: Plan to spend about four to six 45-minute class periods on this project. Allow one class period to hold a class discussion of the United Nations, introduce the activity, and organize students into groups. Allow two or three class periods for students to research a country. Allow one class period for students to take part in the mock Security Council meeting. You may need an additional class period to discuss the Security Council meeting's resolution.

Scale of Project: You will need enough room for students to work in small groups and to hold a mock Security Council meeting. If you wish to invite other teachers and classes to attend the meeting, reserve space in a larger area of the school such as the cafeteria or auditorium.

Group Size: Have individuals or pairs of students represent the 15 member-nations of the Security Council. Students will act as the council's permanent members: the United States, the United Kingdom, the Russian Federation, France, and China. You or the students will need to determine the present 10 remaining members of the council, who are elected to revolving two-year terms. If North Korea and South Korea are not currently part of the Security Council, you should have two students or pairs of students represent them at the meeting. Although the two countries should express their interests, they will not have voting power if they are not currently a part of the Security Council.

Materials: Students may use cardboard name tags to identify the country they are representing. If students have access to a video camera, television, and videocassette recorder (VCR), you might want to have student volunteers tape the mock Security Council meeting for later review.

Resources: Have students use their textbooks, the Internet, the library, and any other materials that you provide to complete their research. Inform students that the UN World Wide Web site (http://www.un.org/) provides information about the activities of the Security Council. Encourage students to explore and tap all available sources of information.

Preparation: Before starting the project, make copies of the Planning Guidelines and Project Task Sheet; you will need at least one copy for each student or pair of students. You may also wish to make copies of the Standards for Evaluation form—which is a project-specific rubric—for students to use in preparing their roles in the mock UN Security Council meeting.

IMPLEMENTATION

1. Give students an overview of the activity by describing its four stages. Tell students that they will first participate in a class discussion about the United Nations. Then students will research the stance toward nuclear proliferation of a particular member-nation of the UN Security Council. Next, students will hold a mock Security Council meeting. Finally, the class will discuss whether the Security Council is effective at solving international crises.

2. To begin the class discussion of the United Nations, ask students to review Section 1 of Chapter 23, entitled "Collective Security." Ask students to describe the main mission of the United Nations. *(maintain world peace)* Then have them identify the six main divisions of the United Nations and explain how each division promotes the UN's mission. *(General Assembly: decides budget, general policy issues, and who sits on councils; Security Council: investigates international disputes and decides on actions to take to promote peace; Secretariat: manages day-to-day operations of UN; International Court of Justice: hears and gives opinions on legal disputes between countries; Economic and Social Council: supervises efforts to improve people's lives; Trusteeship Council: administers trust territories)*

3. Ensure that students understand the following terms: collective security, interdependence, refugee, international law, economic sanctions, nuclear proliferation, and trade embargo. If necessary, have students use the Glossary at the back of the textbook or a dictionary to write the definitions of these terms.

4. Organize the class into 15 to 17 groups of roughly equal size. Assign each group to play the role of one of the members of the UN Security Council, North Korea, and South Korea. Distribute copies of the Planning Guidelines and Project Task Sheet to each group and, if you wish, copies of the Standards for Evaluation form. Go over the instructions to make sure that students understand the assignment. If you have not already determined the current elected members of the Security Council, have students use the Internet or the school library now to determine which countries make up the remaining 10 members. Also have students determine which nation now is acting president of the Security Council.

5. Have students begin their research. Tell students that they should determine their assigned country's position on nuclear proliferation. Students should also learn how the UN Security Council has dealt with the issue of nuclear proliferation in the past and what actions it might take to prevent future nuclear proliferation. Students should prepare a two-page report that summarizes their assigned country's stance on this issue and what actions should be taken to address nuclear proliferation.

6. Once students have completed their research and reports, have students hold a mock UN Security Council meeting. Arrange desks in a large circle so that all students can participate in the discussion. Have students fill out name cards with their assigned country's name and display these on the front of their desk. The nation serving as president of the Security Council should explain the crisis and have South Korea and North Korea first present their views. Then member nations should express their views and recommend a course of action. Have the president or a note-taker write the recommendations on the chalkboard as

they are suggested. After all nations have expressed their views, have them vote on a resolution concerning the issue. The Security Council must have at least nine votes in favor of the agreed-upon resolution, including favorable votes from all five permanent members of the council.

7. After the Security Council has decided on a course of action, have students discuss the outcome. Ask students whether they think the resolution will have a positive impact on collective security and world peace.

ASSESSMENT

1. Use the Standards for Evaluation form to help you evaluate student participation in the mock UN Security Council meeting.

2. Individual grades can be based on the student's role in the Security Council meeting.

3. An option for additional individual assessment is to have students write a short report analyzing their assigned country's stance on nuclear proliferation.

4. Alternatively, you can assess student performance by using any or all of the following rubrics from the *Alternative Assessment Handbook* on the *One-Stop Planner CD-ROM:* Rubric 1: Acquiring Information, Rubric 11: Discussions, Rubric 12: Drawing Conclusions, Rubric 14: Group Activity, Rubric 16: Judging Information, Rubric 18: Listening, Rubric 24: Oral Presentations, Rubric 30: Research, Rubric 42: Writing to Inform.

PLANNING GUIDELINES

The tense situation between North Korea (Democratic People's Republic of Korea) and South Korea (Republic of Korea) has just gotten worse. The North Korean military has massed thousands of troops on the border with South Korea. In addition, an international organization has evidence that North Korea has the materials to detonate a nuclear bomb. If true, this would be a clear violation of the Nuclear Nonproliferation Treaty of 1968. Fearing an imminent invasion, South Korea has asked the United Nations Security Council to take action to prevent a North Korean attack. Meanwhile, North Korea claims that the new troops are only replacements. It has denied having the capability to launch a nuclear attack on South Korea.

The nations on the UN Security Council must act quickly to assess this tense situation and preserve peace. As a member of the council, you will present your country's opinion of North Korea's troop movements and possible possession of a nuclear device. You will also offer your recommendations for how to resolve the dispute. Remember that the Security Council has the authority to take the following actions to promote peace: send peace-keeping forces to reduce tensions, impose economic sanctions, recommend that a nation be expelled from the United Nations, or take military action.

PROJECT TASK SHEET

As part of the mock Security Council meeting, you will choose one of the countries below to represent. You will need to research your country's opinion of troop movements and nuclear proliferation and also how the UN Security Council has dealt with these issues in the past. Draft a report that summarizes your country's stance and your recommendations for how to resolve the dispute between North Korea and South Korea. Keep in mind the idea of collective security as you prepare your arguments. Then present your ideas at a meeting of the Security Council. The members will propose, debate, and vote on what measures to take to resolve the dispute. The resolution must receive at least nine votes to go into effect, including the approval vote of all five permanent members.

Members of the UN Security Council

Permanent Members:

United States

United Kingdom

Russian Federation

China

France

Interested Parties (nonvoting):

North Korea (Democratic People's
   Republic of Korea)

South Korea (Republic of Korea)

Elected Members:

_____

_____

_____

_____

_____

_____

_____

_____

_____

STANDARDS FOR EVALUATION

EXCELLENT

- The student or group thoroughly discusses the assigned country's position on troop movements and nuclear proliferation.
- The student's or group's recommended solution to the dispute is clearly presented, persuasive, and shows a complete understanding of how to attain collective security.
- The student or group members participate fully in the Security Council meeting.

GOOD

- The student or group accurately discusses the assigned country's position on troop movements and nuclear proliferation.
- The student's or group's recommended solution to the dispute is persuasive and shows a good understanding of how to attain collective security.
- The student or group members participate in the Security Council meeting.

ACCEPTABLE

- The student or group discusses the assigned country's position on troop movements and nuclear proliferation.
- The student's or group's recommended solution to the dispute shows an understanding of how to attain collective security.
- The student or group members participate in the Security Council meeting.

UNACCEPTABLE

- The student or group fails to present the assigned country's position on troop movements and nuclear proliferation.
- The student or group fails to offer a solution to the dispute.
- The student or group fails to participate in the Security Council meeting.